KNOWLEDGE TO POWER

UNDERSTANDING AND OVERCOMING ADDICTION

KAL RISSMAN

outskirts
press

Knowledge to Power
Understanding And Overcoming Addiction
All Rights Reserved.
Copyright © 2018 Kal Rissman
v3.0

The opinions expressed in this manuscript are solely the opinions of the author and do not represent the opinions or thoughts of the publisher. The author has represented and warranted full ownership and/or legal right to publish all the materials in this book.

This book may not be reproduced, transmitted, or stored in whole or in part by any means, including graphic, electronic, or mechanical without the express written consent of the publisher except in the case of brief quotations embodied in critical articles and reviews.

Outskirts Press, Inc.
http://www.outskirtspress.com

ISBN: 978-1-4787-9501-8

Cover Photo © 2018 thinkstockphotos.com. All rights reserved - used with permission.

Outskirts Press and the "OP" logo are trademarks belonging to Outskirts Press, Inc.

PRINTED IN THE UNITED STATES OF AMERICA

Acknowledgments

The insights in this book have been gained by working with thousands of addicted persons and their families. I am indebted to all of these beleaguered but brave individuals who shared their struggles and their triumphs with me. They have taught me a lot.

I would like to thank my colleagues at the inpatient treatment center, Jim Wineski, Al Adams and Bruce Perkins. We had some days working together that I will never forget and I am very proud of the work that we did together to help recovering people. I not only learned from these men, but I would trust them with my life.

I am grateful to my former supervisor, the Rev. Doctor Robert F. Maltzahn who taught me many things, but mostly taught me to be both Godly and human.

I owe a debt to David and Carol Shears for their technological assistance in getting this book in print and for supporting me in the project.

I have appreciated the chaplain interns that I supervised over the years, especially Sheryl Maupin and Stephanie Rhodes. These students encouraged me to write down some of the practical wisdom gained in working with addicts for so many years.

Thanks to Judy Urban who gave me tips on publication and has supported my writing efforts.

I am especially thankful for my family of origin and also my family of creation. They have always been supportive of me and provided me with rich examples for this book as well.

I would also like to thank the parishioners in my two congregations who have always treated me so well and have supported this effort as a way of helping congregations to deal with addictions.

I thank my wife, Deborah for her patience and support.

I appreciate the encouragement and support from both of my secretaries, Marilyn Pierce and Julie Horn.

Table of Contents

1	The Disease	1
2	The Spiritual Disease	11
3	Feelings Disease	22
4	Painful Feelings	31
5	Guilt	38
6	Shame	49
7	Anger	60
8	Fear	68
9	Grief and Loss	80
10	Codependency	93
11	Adult Children of Dysfunction	105
12	Family Roles	122
13	Enabling	131
14	Diagnosing Addiction	140
15	Intervention	158
16	Cross Dependency	169
17	The Role of Religion in Recovery	176
18	Relapse	185
19	Having a Program	192
20	Prevention	198
21	Working with addicts	204
	Conclusion	208

1
The Disease

I work in a hospital in the middle of America in Muncie, Indiana, which is very much the average city. In fact, when studies are done of American cities, folks come to Muncie to do their studies. Muncie, Indiana has been called Middletown, USA, because it is such a representation of average cities.

It seems surprising that in such an average city there would be so much drug abuse. You might expect that in New York City or L.A. or Chicago, but not Muncie. About three months ago at our hospital we had 16 overdoses in a two day span one weekend. Four of these people were dead on arrival. About a month ago we had another 14 people who overdosed, two of whom were dead on arrival.

Apparently, there was a new batch of heroin that had arrived in the city that had been mixed with a synthetic narcotic, Fentanyl. This mixture was much more powerful than the addicted persons were used to and they were dying right and left. The drug overdoses and deaths were certainly a hot topic, not only in the *h*ospital, but around the city as well. I spoke to one nurse who seemed exasperated and outraged at this senseless loss of life. She said, "I just can't understand how people can be so stupid to keep using drugs when they know that people are dying".

This is the kind of sentiment that a lot of people have when it comes to trying to understand chemical dependency. People tend to think that chemical dependency is either: a lack of brains, a lack of willpower or a lack of moral fiber.

Unless people have a firm understanding that chemical dependency is a disease, they will never be able to look at it in any other way than a judgmental one. Unfortunately, this never helps anybody to get well.

The Big Book of Alcoholics Anonymous says that addiction is "cunning, baffling, and powerful". My purpose in this book is to hopefully, make the disease a little less baffling. I believe that if people understand what the disease is and what it needs, then we will be able to combat it.

I have worked with this disease for 37 years and have gained some insight that I hope will be helpful to people who work with addictions. I believe that social workers, nurses, physicians and just regular people could benefit from a better understanding of addiction. Probably some background about who I am might be helpful in understanding where I'm coming from.

My background is a little bit unusual. I became an ordained Lutheran minister and was interested in chemical dependency, because one of my seminary professors was a recovering addict. I also have family history of addiction with my grandfather being an alcoholic. Most people who do work with addictions have a vested interest in the disease, it seems. My first Parish was in Jamestown, North Dakota and it was only a part-time position in a mission congregation. Consequently, I had time to work at another job or get other training. I was eventually accepted at the North Dakota State Hospital as a chaplaincy resident. When asked where I would like to do my chaplaincy work, I replied that I would like to work on chemical dependency. After completing my chaplaincy training I was accepted as a chemical dependency intern. I completed that internship and begin working at an outpatient human service center in the drug and alcohol division.

One day while I was looking at a chaplaincy newsletter, I saw an advertisement for a job opening in Muncie, Indiana. It said that they wanted someone who was an ordained minister, had chaplaincy training and had extensive chemical dependency training and certification. They also wanted 3 to 4 years parish experience. It sounded like they were looking for me! The position was for a spiritual care counselor, which was a combination chaplain and addiction counselor. This position was to work on an inpatient drug/alcohol treatment unit and I did this for 17 years. After this time the treatment center was going to be closed for financial reasons. Insurance companies started to not pay for treatment anymore and of course, if drug addicts and alcoholics have money they wouldn't be using it to buy insurance or pay for treatment, but to buy drugs and alcohol. I switched to become the nicotine dependency counselor for the next five years. After this time, I went back to being a chaplain in the hospital, which is what I still am today. I still do 4 group therapy groups on psychiatry every week and most of these groups are made up of over half addicts. Of course, I also see many individuals who are on medical floors that have addiction problems as well.

If you speak to people about addiction being a disease, they usually will say that it might be called a disease, but it's not a real disease. This then leads them to have a moralistic view of addiction. People who work with addicts must not have this view of them, otherwise they will not be able to help the addicted person. Addicted persons may appear to be very insensitive and do act insensitively, but they are at heart, very sensitive people and will be able to smell condemnation a mile away. I cannot state this strongly enough, that it is important to approach people from a nonjudgmental, non-moralistic stance.

Addiction is a disease and has been recognized by the American

Medical Association since the 1950s as such. In order for something to qualify as a disease, it has to meet certain standards. It must have signs or symptoms that are not signs of some other disease, it must be progressive, chronic, and fatal if left unchecked.

There are many signs and symptoms of addiction, such as: a preoccupation with drinking or using drugs, increased tolerance for the drug, solitary using, using drugs to self-medicate, having blackouts, using drugs to deal with uncomfortable feelings and the morning eye-opener to prevent withdrawal. The number one symptom of the disease of addiction is denial that there is any problem, despite negative consequences.

However, the easiest way to diagnose a problem with drugs or alcohol is by looking at what problems it causes in any major areas of a person's life. If drinking or using drugs causes problems in any of these five major areas: relationships, health, legal issues, financial or job/school, then it is a problem. That which causes problems is a problem and that which never causes any problems is not a problem. That is the simplest way to understand if someone's using is beyond the bounds of normal. We will discuss diagnosing addiction in greater detail later on.

Addiction is basically a brain disease. It is not within the scope of this book to explain all of the biochemistry that makes up this brain disease, but it is important to recognize that this is a disease like other diseases such as: heart disease, diabetes, and cancer. There is something that actually changes in the brain chemistry itself and this change is permanent. The addicted brain does not break down chemicals in the same way that the non-addicted brain does. If you put alcohol or drugs in a person who is an addict, the substance that is left in the brain after chemical breakdown is different than if you put alcohol or drugs in the brain of a non-addicted person. The addicted person will have an opioid-like substance left in their brain, which causes the phenomenon of craving. People who do not have that sense of craving have a difficult time understanding the physical compulsion and mental obsession that leads to using more drugs or alcohol.

This is the other element that something must have in order to be considered a disease, namely, loss of control. Lack of power is another way of saying loss of control. In every disease there must be some element that is out of control, otherwise you don't have a disease. In other diseases you see this same loss of control. In heart disease, the rhythm of the heart is off or the muscle itself is not pumping correctly. In diabetes, the body is not handling sugar in the way that it should. With stomach flu there are a lot of things that are out of control, such as vomiting and diarrhea.

It does not do a lot of good to tell someone who is out-of-control in their disease to use their willpower, because that is what they do not have. That is what the disease has knocked out. For example, my mother-in-law has diabetes and I don't think it would be very helpful to her to tell her to use her willpower when eating ice cream and cookies and to not let her blood sugar get out of control, because that's what she cannot do. If she could do that, she would not be a diabetic.

Let's take an example of a disease that we may have all had. Let's use stomach flu as our disease. I would like you to imagine that you have the flu and that you are about as out-of-control as you have ever been. You are sitting on the toilet and you have grasped the garbage can in front of you, because you are not sure whether you are going to vomit, or have diarrhea, or both. Your spouse comes to the doorway of the bathroom and sees you in this out of control condition and then admonishes you by saying, "Hey, don't let that diarrhea fly out your back end; you will deplete your electrolytes. Also, quit the power- puking or you will get dehydrated." She ends by saying "use your willpower, that's what I would do." What would your reaction be to these statements? Wouldn't you be exasperated and say "I would do that if I could"?

So, when we think back to the people that I mentioned before who had overdosed on heroin it is not appropriate to say that they were too stupid to quit using, but rather that they are too out of control to stop using. Actually, on an average, addicts have a higher I.Q. than the national average and my own observation in working with addicted persons bears that out.

So, it is not the I.Q. or Intelligence Quotient that is the problem for addicted persons, but it appears to be something that has come to be called the E.Q., which stands for Emotional Quotient. This is a term that was first used by Wayne Payne in 1986 to describe the emotional development of children.

The Emotional Quotient is the measure of how well a person can handle their own emotions and could be thought of as a measure of how mature a person is. The description of this ability is described in the following statement. The Emotional Quotient is "the capacity to be aware of, control and express one's emotions, and to handle interpersonal relationships judiciously and empathetically".

An interesting facet of this Emotional Quotient is that there are many people with a higher I.Q. that are working for a person with a lower I.Q., but a higher E.Q. In other words, it may be nice to be very intelligent, but that does not guarantee that you will be successful in your life's endeavors or that you will be happy and fulfilled in that life. Having a high E.Q. seems to be much more important to a life well lived than a high I.Q.

Not surprisingly, addicted persons have been tested in various experiments and were found to have a high I.Q., but a low E.Q. However, when these same addicted folks were tested later on after some years of a solid recovery program, they were found to have increased their E.Q. scores tremendously. A person's native intelligence may be a fairly static thing, but that person can catch up emotionally with recovery, which is very hopeful news for addicts.

It is too bad that being smart does not help you in being well. You can be smart as a whip and still be sick as a dog. People are not using because they're too dumb to figure out that it is not good for them, but they are using because they cannot **not** use. They are "powerless over drugs and alcohol and their lives have become unmanageable". That is what Step One of the 12 Steps of Alcoholics Anonymous says. Until people understand that, nothing good can happen.

Another important aspect of addiction as a disease is that like many other diseases, this disease tends to run in families and even in certain races or ethnic groups. For example, when I did my addiction counselor training at the North Dakota State Hospital, about 15% of our patient population was Native American. Most of these patients were from the Sioux tribe, but there were some Crow and Blackfoot patients too.

Something that I soon discovered about Native Americans is that their brain chemistry seems to lack the enzymes that deal with alcohol effectively. Like several other diseases that European settlers introduced to the Native American population, such as cholera, syphilis and smallpox, the indigenous population had no resistance to the disease of alcoholism either. It was almost as cut and dried as that if Native Americans did almost any amount of drinking, they would lose control of it and be alcoholic. They simply cannot tolerate alcohol.

I used to watch a lot of old Westerns on television and was always skeptical when the white man would give the Indians some "firewater" and the Indians would immediately start acting wild and stupid. But unfortunately, these old Westerns are pretty accurate. My experience with this population was that they were wonderful people, kind, funny and deeply spiritual, but all you had to do was add alcohol and they were an instant terror. As my colleague, Wally used to say, "Instant butthole – just add booze"! Apparently, it was not Mr. Colt and Mr. Remington that won the west – it was Jim Beam and Old Granddad!

The same kind of thing happens with other diseases and other races of people. For instance, when you hear of a person getting the disease of Sickle Cell Anemia, you almost always think that the person must be African American, because that is the segment of the population that gets that particular disease. We are not sure why this happens here either, but it just is that way.

There are other ethnic groups that seem to have a good resistance to certain diseases. For example, when looking at the disease of alcoholism, Middle Eastern people seem to generally have a good tolerance for alcohol. Orientals, Arabs and Jews handle alcohol well as a rule. Maybe that is why Jesus of Nazareth never talked about alcoholism, because they really didn't have much of it at all in that culture. Genetically, the Jewish people did not have much trouble with losing control of their drinking. In addition to that, there was a very strong social stigma against drunkenness. If you were drunk even one time in that culture, people would say about you, "He is drunk like a Gentile"! It would have been viewed as socially unacceptable, like picking your nose in public – it just isn't done!

There are some other ethnic groups that fall somewhere in between the poor tolerance of Native Americans and the good tolerance of Middle Easterners. People of Irish descent do not seem to have a very good tolerance for alcohol. One Irishman joked that "God created whiskey to keep the Irish from ruling the world". Scandinavians do not have a great tolerance for alcohol, but Germans seem to do a little better in that department. I have a real mixture of ethnic backgrounds including: Native American, Welsh, Norwegian, German and Polish. I suppose that would put me somewhere in the middle of the tolerance scale, tending towards the down side. It is important for individuals to be aware of their ethnic background to know their genetic predisposition towards addiction.

The other factor besides ethnicity that is part of the addiction issue is family background. Diseases tend to run in not only ethnic groups, but families as well. As I stated before, my mother-in-law has diabetes. Three of her five children also have diabetes now. So if you were a member of her family, you would probably want to be very cautious about your diet and watching your sugar intake and getting regular exercise. Both of my parents died of congestive heart failure and cancer. In addition, my father also had blood clots in his left leg. I have already had blood clots in my left leg and am now on blood thinner. It would make good sense for me to also be watching my diet and exercise, because of my family medical history.

For people who have a family history of addiction of any kind, it would be the same thing. They would want to watch very closely, anything that could be addictive, because they are predisposed to addiction genetically. They might be influenced also to addiction behaviorally, from what they watched growing up with addiction in their family.

I was leading group therapy recently and there was a young man, aged 19, who had overdosed on alcohol and Xanax and had attempted suicide by running his car into a telephone pole. He did not remember any of this, however. He said that he was never going to do that again and said he would just stick to smoking pot from now on, because he never had any problems on pot. When I suggested that he could be dependent on pot too, he said he wasn't dependent, because he had smoked it every day of his life and had no problems. I replied that smoking every day of your life sounds like he depended on it quite a bit and that is dependency. He couldn't see it that way. I asked him about his family's chemical use history and he readily admitted that his parents were both alcoholics and drug addicts. They had given him up for adoption at birth, because they couldn't take care of a baby because their addiction impaired them. I strongly urged him to look at his genetic predisposition to addiction and reminded him that if a person has even one parent that is an addict, they are four times more likely to lose control of their chemicals if they ever use any. With two addicted parents the odds go way up on dependency. He seemed unconvinced, but said he would look at it.

As with many things in our lives, both genetics and environment play a huge role in who we are and what issues we have. Another way of saying that is that both nature and nurture have a hand in determining who we are and how we will live our life. With the disease of addiction, there are many people who not only have addiction in their genetic makeup, but also had a powerful example of living an addicted lifestyle from being around their addicted parents. When both of these factors are present, that person is a sitting duck for their own addiction to begin. As we said before, this addiction is not something that they are consciously choosing, it is just something that happens to them because of who they are and how they were raised.

Certainly one thing that parents can do to help their children and that society can do to help children is to raise awareness of the potential for being predisposed to the disease of addiction just like awareness is raised for other diseases. Sometimes if we know what is coming down the road towards us, we can swerve and avoid it. That would certainly be a good thing.

2

The Spiritual Disease

Because the problem in the disease of dependency is a lack of power or loss of control, that is the reason that it is a spiritual disease. What is needed is more power, or as the Big Book of Alcoholics Anonymous calls it, a Higher Power. The individual does not need more knowledge; they need more power than they have. If they had the power to do what they wanted concerning drugs and alcohol or any other addiction, they would have used it. Spirituality is the ability to recognize that there must be more power than I have and the need for a connection to that power source.

Sometimes the term, spirituality is confused with the word, religion, but they are not the same. Spirituality is a much broader, more inclusive term than religion. Every human being is a spiritual being, but not everybody is a religious being. Comparing religion to spirituality is like saying that all Saint Bernards are dogs, but not all dogs are Saint Bernards. One is more inclusive than the other.

We must be spiritual if we are human. There are certain things that make up every human. We must be physical, that is, have some kind of a body. Maybe it is not the one you want, but it is the one that you have. We also have to have some intellect, some ability to think and reason. Again, we may wish that ability was greater, but at least we have some. We also have to have emotions to be human. We have to be able to feel things like happiness, sadness, anger and fear. And finally, we must be spiritual beings to be human. Without the human spirit I guess we would just be zombies walking around. We must have that sense that out there, in here, somewhere, there is something that is beyond ourselves and we want to be in sync with that something and utilize it for good for ourselves.

People have different names for that something that is beyond. They might call it God, Allah, Buddha, Krishna or some other religious name for a deity. The less religious might call it Divine Providence, The Man Upstairs, The Big Guy, Karma, or simply Fate. Others might just refer to that something as Forces in the Universe. But whatever you want to call it, there is something within all of us that recognizes that we are not all that there is in the world or this universe.

Even atheists recognize that there are forces beyond themselves in this world that work for evil and for good. I have spoken to a good many atheists in the hospital, some of whom are very adamant in insisting that there is no God. But it always makes me wonder why they are pushing so hard against what they say is not there?

So, despite efforts to debunk religion and deny spirituality, new research is showing what we already suspected, that our brains are hard-wired for spirituality and always will be. It is an important part of who we are. But more importantly, it is essential for recovery from addictions. Were it not for the need for more power, we would never talk about spirituality, but since the problem is lack of power, we must.

Let's use a comparison between physical power and spiritual power. At one point I had a rock that was sticking up just a little bit in my yard. Sometimes when I would mow the lawn, the blades would scrape on this rock. I finally determined that this problem had to go from my life, so I began to dig around the edges of the rock with my fingers in order to pull it out. I found that the edges of the rock kept going out further and further as I dug. I realized that I needed more power than I had in my bare hands, so I went to the barn and got a spade. I dug along the sides of the rock and I found that it also went much deeper than I had originally thought. I went back to the barn for more power, bringing back a wrecking bar and a log for a fulcrum to pry that rock up. When that didn't work either, I finally went in the house and called my neighbor, Leon. Leon has a backhoe on his tractor and was glad to come over and dig that rock out and dump it somewhere where it would do no harm.

I knew that I needed more power and when I finally had tried everything I knew, I had to surrender to the fact that I was not getting rid of this problem with my own power. Once I surrendered, I was open to a higher power, namely, Leon's backhoe.

This is the same way things work in dependency. When we have tried everything that we can to control our addiction and it hasn't worked, then we can be ready to surrender to a Higher Power than ourselves.

The question then is; what kind of things could be a Higher Power? The answer is; anything that has more power than I do by myself, up to and including God. For example, a group of people has more power together to help than one person alone. So, a person's group in treatment is a Higher Power. The treatment center with its staff and program is a Higher Power. A person's Alcoholics Anonymous, Narcotics Anonymous, Gamblers Anonymous, Overeaters Anonymous or other 12 Step group is a Higher Power than a person alone. A sponsor from a 12 Step group is a Higher Power as well. For those who have religious background, a supreme being, such as God, might be a Higher Power.

In fact, I would see God working through all of those people, groups and fellowships to get to me. However, you don't have to believe that for the other Higher Powers to work. Whether we believe in God or understand God at all doesn't diminish His ability to help through others. It is like the fact that I really don't understand electricity either, but it doesn't stop me from turning on switches and expecting the lights to come on. I don't have to always understand it - I just appreciate it.

However, if we go back to my example of the rock in the lawn, there is something very important about having more power to do what needs to be done and that is surrender. Until I could surrender and admit that everything I had done would not work, I was not open to tapping into the real power source that I needed, namely, the backhoe. Likewise, until we emotionally surrender to the fact that we cannot be free from our addiction with our own power, or willpower as it is often called, the power source we need is not available to us.

Spiritual surrender is sort of like if you and the Lord were riding in a car together and He says to you, "Look, either you are going to drive or I am going to drive, but we're not both going to drive! Now who has the better driving record"? The best response would be "You do Lord" and then let go of the wheel. When we put our brain in neutral and let ourselves be guided by any Higher Power, then we begin to have a chance at recovery.

I remember that we had a young man in our treatment center that was always balking at suggestions made by the staff. A phrase that he used repeatedly was, "Well, I don't think that will work or I don't think I should have to do that." Finally, my co-therapist was exasperated with this lack of surrender and said to him, "You don't think... Why are you worried about what you think? Your best thinking got you in this place in the shape you're in. Do you really want to go with what you think? I could stop any goofy stranger on the street and ask them what they think you should do in your life and they couldn't possibly give you any worse advice than you have given yourself so far. Do you really want to listen to you? You are literally the last person you should be listening to".

When patients used to balk at the way things were being done in the treatment center, we on the staff, used to give them our famous "misery back refund". We would advise them to try it our way for 30 days and if they didn't like the way their life was going at the end of that time, we would gladly refund their misery and they could go live their life the way they used to. It was a tongue-in-cheek offer to help patients move towards surrender of their will and life. After all, what was the worst that could happen if they tried things somebody else's way? We couldn't possibly ruin their life by doing things differently, because they had already taken care of that before they got to us. Once they realized that they had nothing more to lose, but everything to gain, sometimes there was surrender. And yet, this disease is so powerful, that sometimes there was not, and that is the sad part. As the Alcoholics Anonymous Big Book says, "some pursue their delusions to the gates of insanity or death".

Another example of the need for emotional and spiritual surrender is a story I have told to addicted patients. I say to them, "Imagine that you are on vacation in Florida and driving through a section of swamp. You come upon some construction and a dump truck runs you off the road out into the swamp. You get out of your car, dazed and confused. You think you see a gas station up ahead, but it turns out to just be some junk cars dumped in the swamp. As you turn back towards the highway you walk across some ground that looks solid, but as you take a few steps, you find that you cannot pull your feet out of the muck. You try to pull your right foot up, but your left foot then sinks down further. You try to pull your left foot up, but your right sinks lower. At this point you wonder if this is not something that you have read about before, but never seen, namely quicksand! It turns out that it is".

At this point I ask that patient what is the first thing they would do and they almost always answer the same thing - yell for help. But this actually is the second thing you would do. The first thing you would have to do is to recognize that you are stuck and cannot get out with your own willpower. You would not need to ask for help if you could get out of it yourself. You would just scramble out and tell yourself that you were never going to do that again. You also wouldn't waste time wondering how it was that you got into this predicament in the first place, because that really doesn't matter. You are stuck and that is of paramount importance right now. Maybe later on you can speculate on how this all happened to you and how you can avoid a similar fate in the future, but right now you are stuck.

The second thing is that you would be looking for some kind of help to assist you in doing what you cannot do on your own. You wouldn't be too picky about what form this Higher Power than you would be either. If the wind blew a branch near enough so that you could grab it and pull yourself out; that is good enough. If the wind blew some strands of Spanish Moss near you and you could pull out, that would be fine. If some stranger reached a hand through the brush and offered to pull you out, you probably would not ask him where that hand had been. You would just take the hand and get out of the soup. But what if none of these helpful things arrived and something much more dangerous showed up that had some potential? What if a big old alligator came by and turned and swung his big tail in your direction? What might you do? The answer I usually get is that a person might take a chance and grab that tail and let the gator pull you out, especially if it was the only offer they had and time was running short and they were sinking fast.

The third thing you would do comes after you are out of the quicksand. You would then look at what you did to get in there and plan a program so that you would hopefully, never get stuck in the quicksand again. That would be relapse prevention in your program of recovery.

This story describes the shorthand version of the first three steps of Alcoholics Anonymous: 1) I can't handle it, 2) God can and 3) I think I had better let Him. In our swamp story it is 1) I'm stuck, 2) I need help and 3) I'll take whatever help there is. As we said in Chapter One, nothing happens until there is emotional and spiritual surrender.

The great Protestant reformer, Martin Luther once said, "Until a man is nothing, the Lord can make nothing out of him". If that is true (and it is), it is never more true than when talking about addictions. That is why addiction is a spiritual type of disease.

The foundation on which a spiritual recovery can be built is simple honesty. Until a person can admit how sick they are and what deplorable things they have done to hurt themselves and others, there is no surrender and if no surrender, then no need for a Higher Power and if no Higher Power, then no recovery.

As staff members of the treatment center, we could always tell if a person was making spiritual progress and heading to emotional surrender by how much risk they were taking in their sharing in group therapy. If they were talking about how life wasn't fair and they had a tough break in life, then we knew that they were nowhere in terms of spirituality. If, on the other hand they were sharing how they had hurt other people through their addictive behavior, then we knew that they were on the right track. The more specific an addicted person is in their sharing, the more honest they are being.

So, if a woman in treatment said something like, "Well, I haven't always been as good a wife and mother and daughter as I could be", it sounds like she is admitting to something, but she really is not. She is being too vague and needs to share the specifics. If, on the other hand, she said that she had cheated on her husband three times and had missed the mother/daughter banquet because she was drunk and had not seen her mother for two months, even though she lives in the next block, then she is doing something. Now, she is talking! As we always used to tell our patients in treatment, "If you want to get well, dump your poop in group"! The Alcoholics Anonymous Big Book describes the 12-Step program as being one of rigorous honesty. We will talk more about this when we come to the moral inventory section.

As a rule of thumb, whatever costs somebody something to share is something that will lead to surrender and a spiritual recovery. Sometimes addicted persons who are in treatment will say that they just don't know what it is that they are supposed to be sharing. That is not really true. It is pretty simple - they should be sharing everything that they have never wanted to share with anybody. If they would trot out the worst things that they have ever done and the things that they most want to hide, they will be right on track for recovery. We used to always tell patients, "You have to be willing to look bad if you eventually want to feel good".

If our lives and relationships are not built on rigorous honesty, we really don't have anything. If our relationships are based on lies, deceit, deception and dishonesty, what do we have? We have nothing. Spirituality begins with being honest with who we are and what we have done.

Once a person surrenders their will and life to a Higher Power of some sort and they begin to be honest with themselves and others, spiritual growth always begins to happen. There are certain predictable phases of this spiritual growth and it is good for recovering people to know that these phases are normal, because they do feel very abnormal when they are happening.

These stages will only occur if a person is working a good recovery program, however; they don't just happen because time passes.

The first benchmark is at about three months of recovery. I call this one the "I've-got-it-whipped" stage of recovery. This is a time when a recovering person feels good about not indulging their addiction for several months and they are starting to be proud of themselves. They have not had enough time for bad feelings to pile up yet and seem to be sailing along very nicely. That in and of itself is not a bad thing, but sometimes this good feeling starts to lean towards a sense that the battle is over and the person is all done with struggling with that addiction, hence the "I've-got-it-whipped" tag for this phase. Recovering folks tend to get a little cocky at the three month sobriety mark and are in danger of relapse, because they may stop doing some of the things that got them there. They may start to think of themselves as recovered instead of recovering, which is an ongoing process that needs work every day.

One of the smartest things I ever heard about recovery came from a recovering man who was a big dairy farmer in my first parish in North Dakota. He said to me one day, "Kal, do know the tough thing about staying sober"? "Well, yeah", I said, "I know a lot of the tough things about staying sober, but I'm curious, what do you think it is"? "It's like milking cows", he said, "They never stay milked. There is work to do every day". That really says it all, doesn't it? It's not that a dairy farmer doesn't know how to milk cows. This man grew up on a dairy farm and began milking his father's cows when he was 10 years old and now has been milking his own for thirty years. He knows how to milk cows, but the hard part is that he has to get up and do that every morning and that night he has to do it all over again. The next morning he faces the same task. He can't just pull on their udders real hard and then leave for the weekend! He has to keep at it every day. The consistency of doing the next right thing every day is the key.

The next plateau of a spiritual recovery is at about 6 months. I call this stage the "this-ain't-worth-it" stage of recovery. At 6 months usually a lot of frustrating, irritating things have happened in life, like they do to everyone. But the addicted person has not really had enough time to learn to deal with these feelings from the inside out by talking about them and receiving support from others. On the other hand, there has not been the temporary relief of dealing with feelings from the outside in either. When there is no drinking, drugging or other addictive behaviors, things start to pile up emotionally. It is a time when there is no dealing with feelings in the old, sick way, but there is not yet enough skill and practice to deal with things the new, natural, healthy way. It is a caught-in-the middle kind of time and not very fun.

In the "this-ain't-worth-it" stage people can complain that they actually felt better when they were using their addictive agent and that will be accurate. They probably did feel better then than they do now. But this stage of healing must be somehow gotten through to get to the good stuff that is beyond this. Many addicts relapse during this very difficult time of healing.

The next station along the route of recovery is the one year stage. I call this the "Sodom and Gomorrah" stage of recovery. It is kind of like the Old Testament story of Abraham leading his nephew, Lot and his family out of the wicked cities of Sodom and Gomorrah to safety. Lot's wife turned back to look at the cities from which she had come and turned into a pillar of salt.

For some recovering people at the one year mark, there is a kind of wistfulness to look back at their old using way of life and wonder. Was it really that bad? Is this new life of recovery really going to be that good? They start thinking about the old using friends they have had to leave behind and the fun parties and adventures they used to go on when using and wonder if they will ever be able to feel that kind of excitement again with a new lifestyle. Sometimes they look back and linger too long and turn into a pillar of salt (or turn into a user again).

The good news, however, is that the next phase of recovery can really be amazing. At about eighteen months to two years of recovery if a person has been working a good program, there is usually a tremendous upswing in positive spirituality. Things start to make sense. The ability to let things go becomes much easier. There is a much better defined sense of who one's Higher Power is and a reliance on that power to take care of things. The ability to handle feelings and problems from the inside out instead of from the outside in gives a person the confidence that this new life is going to be good and there might even be enjoyment well beyond what they might have had if they had not become addicted.

One of my recovering colleagues said, "I'm glad I became a drug addict and alcoholic". Someone asked him if he meant that he was glad that he was in recovery. He responded by saying, "No, I'm glad I am an addict, because without that I never would have found a spiritual way by which to live in recovery and this is a blast. I might have gotten through life putting one foot in front of another, but I would never have found this exciting, fulfilling way to live". Now that is a positive spirit!

Sometimes during this period of spiritual growth, there is a desire to enhance the spiritual growth even more by trying some religious things. For example, my dairy farmer friend in North Dakota approached me about 20 months into his recovery and wanted to talk about church. He said, I'm thinking about maybe going to church to help my spiritual growth and I'm thinking about coming to your church, since you know about alcoholism. What do you think? Do you think the roof would cave in if I showed up in your church some Sunday? "No", I replied, "the roof has some really big beams and I think it would be just fine if you dropped in".

He did come to church and then started coming regularly. He said to me after a few services, "You know, I went to Sunday School a little bit when I was a kid, but those stories sure sound different to me now". "Do you think we changed the stories since you were a kid", I asked? "No, I think maybe I'm just different now", he concluded. I think he was right - he was different now and he heard the message of God's grace instead of God's judgment. By the time I left that position, he had become the president of the congregation. There was something down to earth, humble and real about his relationship with God. He was still a little rough around the edges, but the congregation resonated to his genuine faith. They sensed that he had had a spiritual awakening and was authentic in his relationship to his Higher Power.

3

Feelings Disease

In the last chapter we looked at addiction as a spiritual type of disease. But addiction is also a type of feelings disease. The way that people get entangled in the web of addictions is because addictive agents are able to change our feelings and do it in a hurry. If addictive agents such as alcohol, drugs, gambling, food, sex and I-phones did not change the way we feel, people would not be interested in them and would not engage in them repeatedly.

For example, if drinking six cans of Budweiser gave you the same feeling as drinking six big glasses of tomato juice, who would ever be interested and obsessed with Budweiser? The answer is "nobody". But there is something in that Budweiser that can change the way a person feels that all the tomato juice in the world can't duplicate.

When people try to tell you that they really enjoy drinking, because they like the taste of alcohol, you already know that they are kidding themselves. Alcohol is a drying agent and the higher the alcohol content in a drink, the more it dries out our mouth and mucous membranes. They may like the taste of some of the other ingredients in a beverage, but not the alcohol. Usually, the lower alcohol content beverages like beer and wine do have a better taste, because there is less alcohol in it. If somebody really liked the taste of alcohol, they should get the full effect of the taste by drinking some Everclear or moonshine or something that is very high in alcohol content.

What folks really mean is that they like the effect of alcohol and have learned to associate the taste with the effect they are going to get. They know that the stronger the taste of the alcohol, the quicker they are going to get a buzz. It is that buzzed feeling that is most sought after in drinking.

You can see the same thing in any of the other addictive agents. If somebody is smoking marijuana and tells you they like the taste of it, you really have to wonder. Do they really mean that they like the taste of smoke? No, what they mean is that when they feel that smoke enter their lungs, they know that the relaxed, don't-give-a-darn feeling is on its way and their feelings of anxiety and pressure are going to melt away in a haze of smoke for a little while.

Other addictive agents function similarly. According to my intervention specialist friend, Bruce Perkins, the fastest growing addictive agent among younger people today is computer/game/I-phone addiction. There are people who never leave the house and just sit in front of their computer or gaming devices all day. The Smartphone is simply a device where you can leave home, but take your computer and games along with you. I was sitting in a restaurant recently and across from me was a nice-looking young family comprised of a mom, dad, son and daughter. All four of them had their I-phones out and were busy swiping them and touching them. They could barely take time out to give a quick order to the waitress. When their food came, they were eating with one hand and swiping their phone with the other. I watched them throughout the meal and not once during the entire time, did they look up and have any conversation with one another. I don't know if this is the way all of their family time together goes, but if it does, that strikes me as an addiction problem, because it is damaging their relationships. The computers, games and phones all let people go numb for a while and be entertained for a bit. In short, they change the way we feel, just like any other addictive agent.

Similarly, with a gambling addiction, our brain makes its own "feel good" chemicals such as the endorphins and adrenaline in a similar way to the computer, game and I- phone addictive process. This also holds true for spending addictions.

All of the addictions work the same way, namely, they change the way we feel and do it very quickly. If they did not do this, they would not be attractive. It is important to remember that it is not really what happens to us in life that is important – it is how we feel about what happens to us that is important. So, if we can find some way to change the way we feel, that looks like the way to go.

Oftentimes our addictions start when we are fairly young, because at that time we have not yet developed much emotional strength. Emotional strength comes from dealing with feelings over and over in a healthy, natural way, which consists of acknowledging our feelings, sharing them with someone and then leads to being more ready for the next emotional struggle that comes along with growing up.

Being an adolescent is a time when we have a roller coaster ride of emotions and issues. As my colleague, Jim Wineski used to say, "Adolescence is a time that God gave everybody to be nuts for a while". We wonder who we are. We may try out different personas to see which is better accepted. We try to distinguish ourselves from our parents. In fact, there comes a time when we are even embarrassed to be seen with our parents, especially when they seem to be in the "too-stupid-to-live" category. We try to figure out what our identity is going to be among our peers. Am I going to be a stud, a wallflower, a genius, a geek or what? How will I ever get the courage to ask good-looking girls out? Will I ever be asked out? How can I relax enough to look confident? What if I say something stupid and they never let me forget it?

If there was just some magic pill that could make me feel smart and funny and sexy and gorgeous! And then sometimes we find out that there is a magic pill or a magic drink or a magic joint or something that will make us feel very differently than we have been feeling. For young people who have not built much emotional strength, finding something that changes feelings in a hurry seems like a godsend. There is nothing more important to adolescents than the need to belong, to fit in and feel accepted. Drinking and using drugs is the fastest and easiest way to make that happen.

Adults are often surprised that young people would ever start using drugs, drinking or smoking because there is so much information out there now about the dangers of addictive agents. As one perplexed parent asked me, "Why in the world would kids even think about doing drugs when they have these ads on television all the time telling all the bad things that will happen?"

Part of the answer to that question is that young people don't have much experience with death and disaster, like older people do. This leads to a feeling of invulnerability in youngsters. They are bulletproof and don't believe they can be killed. That is why the military wants young men and women in their late teens and early 20's. They can be in a fire fight and see guys dropping all around them and still be saying inside their own heads, "That won't happen to me". It explains why teenaged drivers put the pedal to the metal and careen around sharp turns and text while driving. They don't think they can be harmed and are genuinely surprised when oftentimes this does happen. If you are talking to someone my age, with a Medicare card already, you don't have to convince them that bad things can happen in this life in a hurry. You don't have to warn them of their mortality – they already feel it every morning when they struggle to get out of bed. But when you are young and strong the thought of your own mortality never enters your head. Death and disease are things that happen to old people and other people.

Compounding the problem is that negative consequences

oftentimes do not show up for a while when somebody first starts using addictive agents. For example, if the first time you ever took a drink of alcohol, you got sick, wound up in the hospital, crashed your parent's car and lost your wallet, it wouldn't take you very long to think, "Maybe this drinking thing is not for me". But that is not the way it usually goes. Usually, the experimenting stage of usage gives pleasant results with no downside. There might be a slight headache the next day, but when you think back to how bold, witty, talented and sexy you were while under the influence last night, it certainly seems like a small price to pay.

I recall one of my recovering friends recounting the first time he ever drank alcohol. He said, "I went to a party out in the country and the kids were all drinking. I didn't want to look like a sissy, so I started drinking along with them. I'll never forget that feeling after those first two beers. I thought to myself, 'where has this been all of my life' and I never looked back. I began drinking at every social occasion there was. I was able to talk to girls when drinking and not just girls, but good-looking girls. I felt powerful, witty and good-looking. I had found what I had been looking for all those years."

So, if we do something that seems to work for us in any area of life, we tend to repeat that behavior. If we drink, drug, gamble, play computer games or overeat and it feels good to us and we don't experience any negative consequences from it, we will invariably do that again.

But the biggest reason as to why young people or any people for that matter would use addictive agents is because they work – for a while. The second part of that statement is very important, however. Addictive agents do make us feel better for a little while, but in order to keep feeling good, we have to keep using more. Sooner or later, these addictive things stop solving problems in our life and start causing problems and by that time it is too late.

However, by the time any problems from using show up in our

lives, we have already come to depend on the effects of those addictive agents and that, my friends is dependency. It is explained right in the term itself, dependency. We have come to depend on chemicals or other agents as our primary way of dealing with feelings and problems. Another term for drugs is "mood-altering chemicals". Again, the reason for the attraction is right in the definition. These chemicals alter our moods and that is what people want. Yet another expression for addiction is the term, "problem usage". That term is self-explanatory also. Problem usage is usage that sometimes causes problems. If it never caused any problems it would not be a problem and could be called "social usage".

It doesn't really matter which of these terms you want to use to describe addiction. The bottom line is that a person is using an addictive agent to solve problems and take care of feelings and it worked for a while, but that solution is no longer working and is now causing more problems than it is solving.

As we said, when people start using addictive agents, there is never a thought that they could lose control of these things, there is only the experience that they seem to be working. For example, when I was in college some of my classmates were categorized by how much beer it would take before they could dance. There were the "two-beer-dance-men", the "five-beer-dance-men" and the "not-enough-beer-in-the-world-dance-men". For some the amount of liquid courage needed to get up and dance was not that great, but for others a feeling of being well-lubricated was essential.

There is little thought that this short-cut method of dealing with feelings will ever get out of hand and cause tragedy, because if there was, folks wouldn't do it. I have never had anybody come up to me as an addiction counselor and say, "Kal, I'm 18 years old now. Do you think if I really worked hard at it that I could become a drug addict by the time I am 21, or would it take me longer than that?" Nobody has a goal in life of becoming an addict; that would be ridiculous, and yet that is what happens over and over again with this sneaky disease.

That is another good reason to not adopt a moralistic stance towards anyone who has the disease of addiction. I have talked to a lot of people over the years who say things like, "I don't have any sympathy for alcoholics and drug addicts, because they bring it on themselves. They choose to have that condition." My answer to that is, "No, they may have made the decision to use drugs, alcohol and other addictive agents, but they didn't choose to lose control of it – that just happened and if they had thought they were going to lose control, they never would have started. They took a shortcut and like many shortcuts, it didn't get them where they wanted to go. They chose to use, but did not choose to lose control and wreck their lives."

The net result of taking emotional short-cuts is that it stunts a person's emotional growth. As we stated earlier, adolescence is a time to work through a lot of emotional issues, but if we keep taking the short-cuts, we never develop the emotional strengths for facing other issues later on.

Again, let's use a comparison between building physical strength and building emotional strength. When I was a youngster on the farm we had a lot of cattle, so we baled a lot of hay. In those days we had to stack the bales on a wagon, which was a struggle when I was young. I could only heist those bales up about 4 levels high. However, when I got to be in college, I could toss the same weight bales up 6 levels high with no problem. What was different? I was. I had grown and gained strength from dealing with those bales over and over again as the years went by.

Now, imagine that I had decided for some reason to just sit in a wheelchair and not do any walking or any work for a few years. Then after that I decided that I would get out of that chair and start throwing bales again on the wagon. What do you think would happen? I would probably fall on my face and could barely get up, let alone handle any bales of hay.

In terms of building emotional strength, this is precisely the same thing that happens to addicted people. The addictive agents that they use are like sitting in the wheelchair and letting that vehicle take them where they want to go. They are not struggling with emotional issues and dealing with them in a natural, positive way, so there is no building up of strength to face other feelings and problems later on.

If a young person doesn't deal with feelings of sadness in a healthy way when their pet dies, how are they going to deal with grief issues when their family members die? If a young person doesn't handle rejection straight up when a girl turns them down for a date, how are they going to be able to handle being rejected for a job later on? If a person doesn't learn to handle their anger at losing a baseball game in junior high, how are they going to be able to handle their anger when their kids disobey later in life?

In short, using addictive agents causes emotional immaturity. A person who has been using for many years may be 40 years old, but have the emotional maturity of a 15 year old, because that is when they started using. Wherever the regular using starts, that's where the emotional growth stops. Adding to this problem is the fact that people who have been using heavily oftentimes are physiologically older than their chronological age. They might be 40 years old, but have the internal organs of a 60 year old, because of damage from drugs. They may also have the energy level of a 60 year old and recovery takes energy, so that is a problem. Thus, you end up with a 40 year old who looks and feels like they are 60, but acts like they are 15.

The process of recovery brings these three ages back closer together. The addict's body heals and they feel less like 60 and more like 40 again. Their emotional growth can catch up remarkably quickly to their actual age as well with a solid program of recovery. They no longer act like 15, but more like 40. When addicts say, "I've got to get it together", what they really mean, whether they know it or not, is that they want their emotional age, actual age and physical age to all be synced up to the same age. They want to feel and act as old as they actually are. They want their fragmented life to be whole. Recovery can do that for them.

4

Painful Feelings

There is a cultural aspect to addiction as a feelings disease as well. In the United States and in other countries now, we don't seem to believe that we should have any painful feelings at all. We have ignored the wisdom of the past that taught us that pain is sometimes useful and even necessary in our lives. There was a time when we looked at pain as a helpful sign that there was something wrong in our bodies that needed attending to. For example, I talked to a man not long ago that said he had fallen off his tractor getting down and hurt his shoulder. He started taking some Vicodin pills that he had left over from a previous surgery and was able to keep farming. However, eventually the pills stopped working as well and he went to the Doctor to get some more. The Doctor insisted that he have some tests done like X-Rays and an MRI. The tests showed that he had a torn Rotator Cuff and needed surgery. That pain that he had was telling him that something was wrong and needed to be fixed, but the narcotic masked the pain, making the situation worse.

The same thing happens with emotional pain as it does with physical pain. We tend to think that we should never experience any emotional pain either. If our girlfriend dumps us, instead of feeling the pain of loss and talking about this loss, we are much more likely to reach into the refrigerator or liquor cabinet to get something to numb the pain. If our children are running around and driving us nuts, taking a couple Xanax seems like the thing to do. If our job is stressful, smoking a joint or two can mellow us out.

Whatever can get rid of physical, emotional or spiritual pain in a hurry is what we look for in this country. I would offer the following challenge to you as proof of what I am saying. I challenge you to watch an hour of network television straight through without getting up for snacks or bathroom breaks and see if you can go that long without seeing at least one or a dozen commercials for **Fast, Fast, Fast Relief** of everything from headaches to hemorrhoids. I'll bet you can't do it, because I've tried. There is fast, fast, fast relief of heartburn, diarrhea, ingrown toenails, aching joints, hearing loss, arthritis, headaches, dry eyes, incontinence, flatulence, dry skin, clinical depression and a dozen other maladies.

We don't believe in working through feelings of pain in the slow, natural, healthy way, no matter what feelings are involved. We want what we want and we want it right now.

Remember who we are as a people. We invented instant breakfast, instant credit, instant relationships, instant information, instant cash, supersonic jets and microwave ovens. We want things not only quickly, but we want things to be easy. We also invented automatic dishwashers, automatic flushing toilets, automatic transmissions, self-cleaning ovens and even automatic weapons.

In a hospital setting like I work in, the aspect of pain management has become extremely important. Pain has now become the fifth vital sign that nurses have to account for in the hospital. Managing pain has become the biggest patient satisfaction score determiner. Doctors, nurses and hospitals are judged in large part by how they help their patients avoid any pain during a hospital stay. If the alleviation of pain is not up to what the patient thinks it should be, there will be a bad score given out for that hospital. Another way of translating that is to say that revenue will be lost and in the competitive world of health care today, an organization can't afford to be losing revenue.

So, what is the answer? It seems pretty straightforward; we, in healthcare have to make sure patients don't have hardly any pain, despite invasive and painful procedures that are done to them. When you cut somebody from stem to stern in an open heart operation, you would logically think that there was going to be considerable pain that goes along with this. However, if it saves a life, the pain is worth it. But, in our current culture, we don't even think we should have much pain from even that kind of invasive procedure.

Then how do we make sure that there is minimal pain? We give drugs and more drugs as needed. And sometimes we give more drugs even after they are no longer needed. I read a statistic recently that said that in the past 10 years in America our use of opioids (pain killers) had increased by 600%. That is a literally staggering statistic.

This reliance on pain killers of one type or another, and this really includes all addictive agents, not just opioids, is seen by most folks now as the only way that one can deal with pain. An example of this comes from a therapy group that I was leading on the psychiatric unit just this week. We were talking about the need to stay off all other drugs, otherwise the anti-depressant drugs and anti-psychotic drugs will not work. Street drugs interfere with the effectiveness of psychiatric drugs. Two of the members of the group became very belligerent and said that they were willing to quit all the other drugs, but there was no way that they were going to give up smoking marijuana. They had all the usual arguments for using marijuana, such as: it is a natural plant, it has medical uses and it relaxes me. I tried to suggest to the one patient that he had come into the hospital after having hallucinations in jail for several days and it would probably not be a good idea to be using a hallucinogenic drug. He said that I was wrong and that was the dumbest thing he had ever heard. The other patient came at the issue from a pain relief standpoint. She said, "I have Lupus and

I have to have marijuana for pain and if you can't understand that, screw you, dude" and she stormed out of the group room.

I never even got to the part about trying to use some natural means of pain control like biofeedback, yoga, neuro-massage, cranial sacral therapy, prayer or meditation. Those things aren't even considered by most of our people in this country.

I asked one of our addicted patients in group therapy to go on a little fantasy trip with me. "Imagine", I told him "that you go to your physician and tell him that you have been quite anxious lately, have had trouble sleeping and have been generally restless. Your Doctor then tells you that he knows a good counselor for you to go see and discuss your worries. He also gives you a new diet and exercise program. He tells you to take a warm shower and read a book before bed as well. He even suggests that if you pray and meditate, you could do that right before your progressive relaxation exercises." I conclude by saying, "Now what would you think of your Doctor"? The patient responded, "Well I'll tell you one thing – I wouldn't go to see that quack again. He should have known from those symptoms that I need Xanax"!

That is what physicians are up against – that kind of quick-fix, no-pain, better- living- through-chemistry thinking. Physicians are taking a lot of heat for over-prescribing addicting medications and certainly some of the blame does fall on them. It might be more accurate to say that a lot of that blame falls on a few of them, because many physicians are very hesitant to give out prescriptions too freely that involve substances upon which people can easily become dependent.

But every area also has some physicians that are known as the "Doctor-feel-goods" of that region. These Doctors believe every malady can be taken care of with some drug and usually it is an addictive drug. In fact, when I worked at the drug/alcohol treatment center, we used to be able to diagnose people with addiction just by the name of their physician. If a patient came to the center and had "Doctor

Feelgood" as her physician, we didn't even have to do an evaluation of her; we already assumed she was an addict and invariably she was.

We have to take into account that our physicians are trained in our culture; the culture that wants everything quick and painless. Before we jump on the physicians too hard, we need to remember that they are simply doing what we want and in many cases, demand. They are giving us what we clamor for and if they don't, we will go to some other physician and then they will have no practice.

Another complicating factor in the medical system is that our physicians are highly trained and go to school for years and years to become a physician. But this requires a lot of money and that money has to come from somewhere. Every year I do a lecture on addictions for our medical residents. I asked them last year what the average indebtedness was for completing medical education in Indiana. They knew right away what it was. They asked me, "In-state or out-of-state"? "What is in-state", I asked? "Two hundred and sixty thousand dollars", they said. "Well, what is out-of-state then", I inquired? Four hundred and forty thousand dollars", they answered. "Some owe more than that and some less, but that is the average", they concluded.

My thought at this juncture was to say, "Well, you had better make some money after you get out of medical school"! That is a lot of money to pay back on student loans. But the insidious part of this situation is to then look at how a Doctor can make a lot of money. One way to make a lot of money is to see a lot of patients, so if you build a big practice, that will help. But the downside is that in order to see a lot of patients in a day, the fastest way to do this would be to write a lot of prescriptions and send the patient on his way and then see the next one. It is very time consuming to sit and listen to each patient and then try to come up with some natural ways for healing to impart to them. It goes a lot faster if you see that there is anxiety to just quickly write them a prescription for Ativan or Xanax. If they have a sore back, writing a prescription for Soma or Vicodin or some other medication goes a lot faster than explaining physical therapy, massage and exercises. Before the physician knows it, he or she has become a "Dr. Feelgood".

I know how easily this happens because I went to my Dentist last year and had to have a crown put on one molar. I like my Dentist very much and trust his work, but when the procedure was done he handed me a prescription for Vicodin and I was very surprised. I didn't have the prescription filled. I don't need Vicodin for a crown on a tooth. I took a couple Tylenol one time after the crown was put on and that was it. There was some pain, but I expected some pain and I have learned to deal with it in natural ways.

I realize that I am fortunate because my parents set a good example of how to deal with both physical and emotional pain in a natural, healthy way and not everybody has that advantage. My father had osteomyelitis when he was 18 years old that left his left hip totally fused. He was told that he would probably never walk again, but he did. He did not walk well or quickly, but he made every step count, because he had pain every day. He was able to farm and ranch his whole life with that hip and that pain and the most I ever saw him take on his worst days was one aspirin. Over the years he developed a threshold of pain that was almost off the charts. For instance, I saw him fall out of the barn and break his ribs and all he said was "That will be a little sore for a while". He also dropped a wagon tongue on his foot and broke the foot. He sucked in his breath and then said, "It's going to be even tougher to get around for a bit". He did not reach in the medicine cabinet for painkillers and did not reach in the refrigerator for beer.

When emotional pain hit our family, like the death of my grandfather, we were shown that it is good to cry, to talk about what we would be missing without grandpa and to listen to music that helped us grieve. Since we lived next to the cemetery, I was allowed to take the loader tractor over and push the dirt into the grave over his casket. I remember this fondly as being one last loving act that I could do for my grandfather, who was a great, joyful and spiritual man.

It would really help if everyone had these kind of experiences like I did growing up, but I am very aware that this does not happen nearly often enough in our culture. Unfortunately, our physicians face far more people who are used to taking shortcuts to deal with their feelings of physical and emotional pain, than people who deal with those feelings in a healthy, non-pharmaceutical way.

As long as physicians are trained in and work in a culture that demands quick relief of pain and easy solutions to problems, there will be pressure to use the prescription pad for everything. From my standpoint, it looks like it will be very difficult to be a physician in this culture as long as we believe in better living through chemistry. I hope that physicians can band together and decide to stop the trend of excessive prescribing of addictive substances for every health problem. I hope that they can apply some pressure against the agencies that score hospitals so heavily on the criterion of pain control.

I believe it would take a change in our entire culture to curb the kinds of addiction problems that are pandemic right now in our country and in our world. But it takes a long time to change an entire culture and a lot of effort and pulling together by various concerned groups to accomplish a task this large.

5
Guilt

There are many feelings that a person can have that can cause emotional pain such as: loneliness, fear, anger, grief, guilt and shame. One feeling that seems to drive addiction more than most would be guilt. Every human has guilt, but addicts have it excessively.

Guilt is feeling bad about what we ourselves do. When we do something that we know we shouldn't or do something bad, we feel guilty. When we make a mistake or screw something up, we feel guilty. The flip side of this coin is when we don't do something that we were supposed to do, and then we feel guilty also. When we neglect to do what is expected of us, we feel guilty. In the Christian church when I grew up these were always talked about as the "sins of commission" and the "sins of omission". It was about doing what we shouldn't and not doing what we should.

The disease of addiction always causes plenty of guilt, because things are done that should never be done and other things are left undone that really should have been done.

The reason this happens is because one of the symptoms of addiction is a loss of values and a lowering of moral standards. Values are things that used to be important like: family, honesty, hard work and faithfulness. These tend to go out the window as the disease progresses.

Morals tend to go downhill as a person gets sicker as well. Things that used to be called "wrong" become business as usual. Things like being abusive physically, verbally or sexually are not uncommon for addicts as they progress in their disease. As one patient on rehab said to me, "When I look back on some of the things I have done over the past few years, I can't believe that it is me, but I did them. I'm just not that kind of person, but I guess I have to face the fact that I have become that kind of person".

As we said before, the attraction to addictive agents is that they do make you feel better for a while. When we drink or use drugs, the inhibitory center of the brain is anesthetized for a while and we are not inhibited and feel like we can do anything - dance, talk to people, take dares and act carefree. The downside is that when the inhibitory center of the brain is knocked out, we are not inhibited from doing things that we really shouldn't be doing. The inhibitory center is the brain's stop sign. It is that thing which prevents us from doing crazy, dangerous things. It is the part of the brain that tells us to wait a minute and think things through. Is this really a good idea? Is the risk going to be worth the reward? Does this action fit in with my values and moral standards? Could this behavior get me in trouble? Could this one moment of excitement cost me for the rest of my life?

Another factor in the lowering of moral standards, which leads to guilt, comes from denial being the number one symptom of this disease. It is essential for addicted persons to cover up their using behaviors, otherwise they can't keep the game going. So, if you ask an alcoholic how many drinks she has had, she is not going to tell you the truth and say, "I've had 15 mixed drinks". She is going to say something like, "Well, I've had a couple" or I've had a few". This is a form of denial known as minimizing. She is not out and out denying that she has been drinking, but she is low-balling the amount to not sound so bad. Over the years, I have learned to interpret what these terms mean when an addict uses them. The phrase "a couple drinks" means eight to twelve drinks and the phrase "a few drinks" means twelve to 18 drinks. Likewise, smoking "a little" pot means two to four joints and smoking "some" pot means four to seven joints.

Yet another form of denial that causes guilt is rationalizing. Rationalizing is giving a reasonable sounding excuse for unreasonable behavior. I remember a man who was in treatment that previously told his wife that he had to go to the bar after work, because his coworkers wanted to congratulate him for being top salesman for the month. He said that he had to stay late and celebrate, because otherwise he would be letting the team down. But the next month when he was not the top salesman, he did the same thing and stayed late at the bar and was knee-walking, pant-peeing drunk when he got home. He told his wife that he had to be a good team member and help another man celebrate being top salesman. According to him, he had a good reason every week why he had to do some extensive drinking. He called them reasons, but his wife called them excuses and gave him an ultimatum, that it was either booze or her. That's when he came into treatment.

One of the more ironic examples of rationalizing was in a group that I was leading in the treatment center. There were two different men in the group, both of whom had children. The first man said that his drinking didn't affect his children negatively because he always went out to do his drinking outside the home, so since the kids didn't see him drinking, it didn't hurt them. The second man claimed that his drinking didn't negatively affect his children for exactly the opposite reason. He said that he drank at home and didn't run around in the bars and because he was always home, his children were not affected. There were two opposite excuses for the same behavior and the fact of the matter is that neither of them sounded reasonable.

Currently, as we said, there is a huge problem with prescription drugs. People try to avoid feeling guilty about excessive drug use by reasoning that anything that comes from a nice, clean pharmacy must be alright. The phrase I hear folks using over and over again is this, "But I got these from my Doctor". "Why would my Doctor prescribe these if they could cause a problem", is the other statement that keeps coming up from people in trouble with prescription drugs? I reminded a woman last week that anything that is mood-altering carries with it the danger of dependency. Your brain can't tell the difference in what you buy in a shiny, clean pharmacy and what you might purchase in a back alley from a shady, burned out drug dealer. All your brain knows is high or not high.

The rationalization for compulsive gamblers is that they have to keep playing to win back what they lost. They just know that their luck is going to turn around, but if they quit too soon, they won't see the turn around. There is also a connection between gambling and drinking. One of the things I noticed on a trip to Las Vegas some years back is that all the drinks are free. Isn't that nice! Not really. The casino owners figured out a long time ago the conspiracy between booze and gambling. It works like this. When we drink, we relax and our inhibitions are gone, so we gamble more freely. When we gamble, we either win, in which case we have to celebrate with more drinking, or we lose, in which case we have to drown our sorrows with more drinking. Of course, when we do more drinking, we gamble even more and the whole cycle starts all over again. This vicious cycle goes until we are drunk and broke.

With computer/game/Smart Phone addiction the rationalizing is that it is not hurting anything. I talked to a young man with a problem in this area and he said, "I don't know why everybody is always ragging on me about my games; it's not like I'm hooked on drugs or booze". The fact that he almost never left the house and was sitting in front of his various gaming devices for 20 hours a day, didn't seem to register with him as a problem like it did his parents.

People with eating disorders usually revert to the rationalization that they have to eat to live and that is certainly true. However, it is the extremes of overeating, starving or eating the wrong things that is not looked at by the person with an eating disorder.

Similarly, folks with sexual addictions usually trot out the rationalizations that sex is a gift of God, a natural thing and it feels good. While all those things are true, the gift of sexuality can certainly be misused and can cause guilt not only for the individual, but for partners that that person may have as well. There is tremendous guilt over sexual misconduct, whether that is unfaithfulness, rape, molestation, pornography or sex with animals.

Another form of denial that causes guilt in addicted persons is blaming. If an addict can push blame onto somebody else, they can avoid being confronted on their disease. It is very important to find other people who are at fault or other circumstances that are to blame. Addicts who are married find this blaming technique as a handy way to keep the heat from themselves and put it on somebody else. When the wife complains about her husband's pot smoking, he replies that the only reason he needs to mellow out so often is because she nags him all the time. As one of my former patients said to his wife, "The reason I smoke is because you bitch all the time. If you didn't do so much bitching, I wouldn't have to smoke so much." Of course, this husband didn't have much of a response when I turned this statement around on him and asked him, "How does your excessive smoking help your wife to be less bitchy?"

The last thing an addicted person wants is for somebody to pin them down as to how much they are using and how many problems this is causing, because then they might have to stop and that seems not only grim, but impossible. Consequently, anything that threatens the usage must be squelched by either simple denial, "No, I don't have a problem with drugs", rationalizing, "I have to take these pills because I have pain", minimizing, "I just had a couple" or blaming, "the problem is that you bitch all the time".

Sometimes rage and abusive language will do the trick to stop all conversation about a need to quit using. I remember one of my former patients who grew up in an alcoholic home said, "We figured out very early on that we shouldn't say anything about Dad's drinking, because it was going to get really unpleasant around the house if we did. Everybody, including mom, tiptoed around the issue of drinking. There was this huge gray animal blocking everything in our home, but nobody dared to observe that there was this elephant in the living room".

I recall one extreme case of denial mixed with anger from when I worked at the North Dakota State Hospital many years ago on the rehab unit. There was a husband who had been court-ordered into treatment because of multiple DUI's. His wife came to family week and said that her husband had browbeaten her and the kids into silence about his drinking many years ago. He would come home from drinking and order everybody in the family to line up in front of the couch and then he would go up and down the line like Adolf Hitler, haranguing, yelling, cursing and accusing one after the other of them until he tired and went and passed out.

The family counselor casually remarked that he would sure like to have a tape recording of that to play in group to help break down his intense denial. Surprisingly, the wife said that she actually had a tape recording of one of his rants. She said she had slipped a tape recorder under the couch when she heard him pull into the driveway and had the whole thing on tape. She brought it in the next day and played it for the staff and it was horrible. It was even worse than what she had described. The staff was excited that surely this new picture of himself on tape would break the denial of that husband.

The next day in family group the tape was played in front of the patient and his group. He sat impassively throughout the tape and when it was all done was asked what he thought about himself. His response was to say, "Well, I don't know who you got to play me in that fake tape, but he didn't sound anything like me at all"! Clearly, this was a man who was going to require some extra work by the staff.

Sometimes the amount of guilt depends on which addictive agent is used. For example, if someone is drinking alcohol, they may have enough extra income to support a habit like that without going broke. However, if they have a crack cocaine habit, it is going to be very difficult to keep up with that financially. Unless a person is independently wealthy or has won the lottery recently, there are only three ways to keep up with a cocaine habit: dealing, stealing or prostituting. None of these behaviors are things to be proud of and you can readily see that tremendous guilt would ensue. I remember listening to the confession of a cocaine-addicted man who tearfully related that he was so desperate for money for cocaine that he sold his two children for ten thousand dollars apiece and then smoked all that money up.

Crimes are committed all over the country to get money to be able to feed a drug habit. I went to a workshop a few years ago and the Drug Czar for Indiana was speaking about addiction and law enforcement. He claimed that 90% of the people in prison in Indiana were there either directly or indirectly because of drug/alcohol abuse. He stated that many crimes were done under the influence of addictive substances and the rest were committed to get money to get more addictive substances. Obviously, people who commit crimes have a high degree of guilt over this.

Guilt over doing crazy and hurtful things while using and the guilt over unlawful and despicable things done to get addictive agents plague the addict's conscience. But this illness keeps perpetuating itself since guilt is one of those feelings that we don't like to experience, and then the guilty person looks for a way to get rid of that feeling for a little while. And what is the quickest way to get rid of any feeling in a hurry? You guessed it - take a mood-altering substance! Then the whole thing starts all over again. There is more destructive behavior while high, then more guilt, and then more chemicals needed to get rid of that guilty feeling. This thing just keeps going round and round until one of these things happens: recovery or else death, imprisonment or insanity.

If an addict is to avoid the grim prospects of death, imprisonment and insanity, there must be an ongoing program of recovery. As we said before, recovery starts with honesty and that means getting honest about what one feels guilty about. Nobody who hangs onto guilt and keeps it buried inside is clean and sober for very long. The poison of the guilt soon invades everything new that an addict might try to start.

The question then becomes, if someone really wants to start a new life, be clean and sober and get rid of their guilt, how would they do that? The answer is pretty straightforward. The cure for guilt is confession and hopefully, forgiveness. Until we get the burden of our misdeeds off our chest, they will continue to plague us. This is not a new revelation. The Christian Church has known for centuries that "confession is good for the soul". In fact, in my denomination we start every worship service with the "Brief Order for Confession and Forgiveness". The church has recognized for a long time that all relationships have to be based on honesty if they are to be real and worth anything.

If an addict is recovering in a 12-step program, there are specific steps set up to deal with the aspect of confession and forgiveness. The 4th step states, "We made a searching and fearless moral inventory of ourselves". This is a process of spiritual stocktaking where we look on all the shelves of our life and see what is actually there for good and for ill. It is a searching inventory in the sense that we look at all of the areas of our life and not just the good areas. It is a fearless inventory in that we look all the way to the bottom of each area and don't just look at the surface material.

One of my functions as Spiritual Care Counselor in the treatment center was to prepare patients for taking a good moral inventory and then to listen to that inventory in the 5th Step. The format was for the patient to have 3 different columns to their inventory. The first column was listed as "Assets". This is the section where the patient would list all of their good qualities. These are the things that they would want to keep about themselves. This is a very important undertaking and it is the first section for a reason. Sometimes after addicts look at all the bad stuff, they can't see anything good about themselves at all, and that just isn't true. So, we start with what's right with them. This may be things like, I have a good sense of humor, I have a good education, my parents still love me, I am still employed, I am good with mechanics, I am organized, I help my neighbors with building projects, I can sing, I am young and I feel things deeply. There are many other assets that a person might have, but it is important for them to know that they don't have to get rid of everything about themselves and throw the baby out with the bathwater.

The next section of the inventory is entitled "Defects". This section is subdivided into maybe a dozen different character defects such as: denial, selfishness, excuse-making, dishonesty, false pride, phoniness, resentments, intolerance, impatience, oversensitivity, self-pity and fear. Under each of these subcategories, the patient will list specific examples that demonstrate that defect of character.

The final section is entitled "Changes". This is the section that holds the plan of what the recovering addict is going to do to take what is wrong and make it right. It is essential that these changes be in the form of measureable, observable actions. For example, it does not do any good to say that I am going to be less selfish in the future. I need to put down the action that demonstrates how I am being less selfish and that I am thinking of others more than myself, and who these folks are that are going to benefit from what I do for them and how often I am going to do this. So, it is much more helpful rather than saying, "I'm going to spend more time with my kids from now on", to have a plan that says, "I will read one bedtime story to my two children every night before they go to bed." That change may not be a huge one, but it is very specific. It will be easy to tell if you are doing it or not. Am I becoming a better dad? Well, did I read them the story every night this week or not? If so, I'm changing; if not, I'm just talking about changing.

The goal of taking a moral inventory is to get rid of the guilt. Instead of having a dark cloud over my head of guilt feelings that I've never wanted to own, when I do an inventory, I drag everything out of the basement, look at it, decide what to keep and what to throw away and make a plan for doing that.

Step 5 is the next step of the 12 Steps of A.A. and this is the verbal sharing of that written inventory. Step 5 says, "We admitted to God, to ourselves and to another human being the exact nature of our wrongs." My job in the treatment center was to be the other human being that listened to the inventory. It really is like a cumulative confession of everything unhealthy that the person can think of from their lives. It is one thing to write down all the stuff I have never wanted to look at, but it is quite another to confess that to another human being. Normally, we like to try to keep all this material between ourselves and God, because we figure He probably won't tell anybody. But when another human being hears this litany of defects it is a very humbling, but cleansing thing.

It is a thing that really dumps a load of guilt off at the door. Another person has heard my worst stuff and they didn't run out of the room, screaming with their hands over their ears. The world is still turning and the lights are still on. I feared that my life would be over if anybody ever heard this story and here is this man just taking it all in and still looking at me as if I were a valuable human being. In short, there is acceptance, which is a tremendous spiritual experience and one that keeps guilt from running and ruining my life.

The same kind of thing can happen at Alcoholics Anonymous meetings as well when honest sharing is done. One of my recovering friends always jokes, "I went to an Alcoholics Anonymous meeting and decided to surrender and I told them all my worst stuff and at the end of the meeting, they all gave me their phone numbers. What kind of fellowship is this?"

6

Shame

The companion feeling to guilt that causes great emotional pain is shame. These two feelings, guilt and shame are often viewed as being the same thing, but they are not. They feel very similar inside of us, but they come from two very different places.

As we said in the last chapter, guilt comes from things that I do or don't do that make me feel uncomfortable. Guilt is about "doing". Shame, on the other hand, is about "being". We can have a tremendous amount of shame and never have really done anything that would be considered very bad. That is because shame comes from what other people have done to us that is damaging and demeaning. So, guilt is what I myself do that has hurt me and shame is what other people have done to hurt me. We can be shamed by our family of origin, by any unhealthy relationships we might currently be in, by society's expectations (body shaming) or even by ourselves when we use shaming statements in our self-talk.

The comparison of guilt and shame is described by the following statements. Guilt is the sense that I have made a mistake. Shame is the sense that I am a mistake. Guilt leads me to believe I have done something bad. Shame is the belief that I am bad. Guilt says that I have screwed up. Shame says that I am a screw up. Guilt is "I did wrong". Shame is "I am wrong".

All forms of abuse and neglect are shaming. If a child is beaten by his or her parents or guardians regularly the shaming message is clear that they must not be worth very much, because if they were, they wouldn't be treated like that. We don't destroy that which we value, so abuse tells kids that they have no value.

If a child is sexually abused, they are being given a strong message that they are dirty and wrong. They probably are given this message verbally as well, so that they won't tell anybody about the abuse. If the child feels dirty enough and worthless enough, they will not tell anyone about the abuse, for fear that people will view them as worse than they already feel. The same thing happens to adults who are raped or sexually abused. They get the message that they are worthless and damaged goods and it doesn't matter what happens to them from this point on.

If a person is verbally abused, especially a child, it has the same effect of giving that person a rich spirit of "nobodiness" and worthlessness. Children don't have enough life experience to know what is "normal" and what is not. To a child, their version of "normal" is whatever they have grown up with or gotten used to. Treatment units and psychiatric units are full of people who have been verbally abused. Phrases like: "What's wrong with you? Are you stupid? Can't you get anything right? How could anybody ever love you? You dumb little sh*#. I wish I had never had you. The best part of you ran down my leg" were heard all too often as they were growing up.

Also, spiritual abuse has a very damaging effect on people. There is a lot of what I call "bad religion" floating around out there and it makes it very difficult for people to feel very good about themselves existentially. People have grown up with words like: "God will get you for that", "No drunkards will enter heaven", "Being a homosexual is an abomination to the Lord" and "If you change your ways, then the Lord can love you". In my work as Spiritual Care Counselor on the treatment unit I used to long for the day that I would get a patient that didn't have any religious background at all, because then at least I wouldn't have to tear down the shaming structure of bad religion first, before I could help them build a positive spirituality.

I have discovered over the years that people who fall under the addiction umbrella as either: addicts, codependents or adult children of dysfunction tend to see themselves more clearly and understand the disease more fully when I use examples, stories and parables. I will share some of these as we go along.

One example I have used in group to get the point across to patients with intense shame issues is the following. I ask the patient, "Imagine that you have an old Dodge Dart automobile and your neighbor asks you if he can use your car to go coon hunting that night". He wants to drive it out in the cornfield along the creek, chew tobacco in it and throw dead raccoons in the back seat as he hunts. Maybe you are not thrilled with the prospect, but you decide that the Dodge is just an old beater and it won't make any difference anyway what he does with it. But now let's imagine a different scenario. Let's say that you have a new Ferrari and your neighbor wants to borrow it to go coon hunting. "What do you say to him?" At this point, the patient always says that he would not let them take the Ferrari. "But what is the difference", I ask? "They are both cars, aren't they"? The response from the patient is always something to the effect that one vehicle has value and the other does not. At this juncture I ask the patient how they have been treated in the past and how they are now treating themselves. Is it more like a Ferrari or more like a Dodge Dart? They get the point. But the conclusion to this story is that people aren't cars and it doesn't matter how much mileage we have on us, we are still valuable – that hasn't changed. We are all Ferraris.

All people have a certain amount of shame. It's not like there are some folks who have lived on this earth and have totally escaped shame. But the concern here is the difference between some shame and having toxic, crippling shame. Shame is a universal experience, but there are some humans who have way more than their share of it and it is devastating. Addiction is a shame-driven disease and unless the shame is dealt with, there will be no lasting recovery. Shame is to feel as if one is a failure and is somehow flawed and lacking in whatever it takes to be a decent human being. Ultimately, to be filled with shame is an experience of nothingness.

For people with Christian background, there is a story in the beginning of Scripture that does a beautiful job of talking about the origin of shame and what shame does to our relationships. If you don't have Christian background, the story is good enough to stand on its own merit as a way of understanding human nature.

The story comes from the 3rd chapter of Genesis right after the creation story with the first man, Adam and the first woman, Eve in the Garden of Eden. The Hebrew word for Adam translates to "mankind" and the Hebrew word for Eve translates to "womankind", so this story is not just about two ancient people, but is a story about all men and all women for all time.

As the story begins, the Lord God has created a perfect environment in which the humans can live, the Garden of Eden. There is just one rule and that is for the people to not eat the fruit from the tree in the middle of the garden. That seems pretty easy, because they don't need it and have everything they need without it. But of course, which tree are they then attracted to? That's right, the one they shouldn't have! This is starting to sound familiar isn't it?

The serpent speaks to the woman and says, "Did God tell you that if you ate of the fruit from that tree in the middle of the garden that you would die?" "Well, yes He did", the woman responds. "No", the serpent responds, "you won't die; you will be like God, knowing good and evil". That was the temptation that was too great to turn down. It also signals what is our problem still today, namely, that the creature is never satisfied with being God's good creation. The creature wants to be the Creator. Humans want to be the captain of their own ship and the master of their own destiny. We would like to be our own god.

The woman ate the fruit and gave it to her husband to eat and he partook also. Then their eyes were opened and they realized that they were naked. They sewed fig leaves together to cover up. Later on, the Lord came walking in the garden in the cool of the evening and said, "Adam, where are you (as if He didn't know, being God)"? Adam said, "We hid ourselves because we were naked". "Who told you that you were naked"? The Lord wants to know where they got the idea that they, literally of their naked selves, the way He created them, were not o.k. In other words, "What made you think that you had to add something to yourselves, like fig leaves, to be acceptable? Did you eat of the fruit that I told you not to"? Adam's response makes me wonder if he wasn't maybe an alcoholic, because it is filled with blame. "The woman that you gave me; she gave me the fruit and I did eat". Adam blames not only his wife, but he actually blames God for giving him this woman. Eve's response makes her sound like a good codependent as well with some blaming of her own. She says, "It was the serpent! The serpent gave it to me and I ate".

Then the Lord told them the consequences of their disobedience. They had to leave the perfect garden. They had to work for a living. They had to have pain, sickness and eventually, death. It was a big price to pay for wanting to be their own god and for disobeying.

This story powerfully demonstrates what shame is all about. When we have damaging shame, we always believe that we either have to add something or take something away from ourselves to be acceptable. We are never alright just as we are. With the advent of shame, Adam and Eve realized that they were naked and that their nakedness was not alright and they had to use a defensive strategy of sewing together some fig leaves to cover up. Even today, little children like to run around naked until the time that they have had enough shaming messages from adults that they need to add some clothing to be acceptable.

There are billion dollar industries based solely on the need to cover up shame. The not so subtle messages from Madison Avenue advertising tell us that we might be attractive if we could just lose 45 pounds and here is the product that can help you do that. We could feel confident if we just could get rid of that acne, that sagging flesh, those brown spots, the turkey neck, the thinning hair, the unwanted hair and the spider veins. There are so many things that we need to have less of to be alright.

There are also many areas where we need to have more than what we have. We need to have more muscles, larger breasts, a bigger brain, a fatter wallet, a larger house and more fashionable clothing. Many people would probably disagree with me, but I personally think that the current fad of getting tattoos and piercings is an attempt to relieve shame. It is another example of adding something to me to be just a little more cool than I actually am. It says that I am not o.k. just the way God made me and I need to add something more.

There are even some procedures that can both take something away and add something to make us more desirable. For example, if a woman could have some fat sucked out of her butt and injected into her lips, she could look more like actress, Angelina Jolie!

The net result of all of this shame is that we end up feeling that we are bad. If we are bad, we need punishment in order to wipe the slate clean and feel good for a little while. This explains why people who have shame settle for poor relationships and oftentimes, abusive relationships.

I talked to the parents of a young woman who was in an abusive relationship with a boyfriend. Her parents were mystified that this bright, beautiful daughter of theirs could wind up with one loser boyfriend after another. They said that she had a decent boyfriend one time, but she quit going with him after only a short while and then took up with what they called "another dirtball".

I immediately knew that there had to be some kind of abuse when this young woman was younger to give her this kind of poor self-image and the decision to settle for less than she should have. Through the course of treatment, we eventually discovered that she had indeed been sexually abused by an uncle and never told anybody about this and now the uncle was dead. After this period of abuse she said that she had always felt "dirty and worthless".

It all made sense then in a sick kind of way. Her self-image was so poor that she didn't believe that she deserved any kind of healthy relationship with a decent man. When she did accidentally go out with the one healthy boyfriend, she said that she felt horribly uncomfortable and unworthy next to him, so she dumped him in a hurry. In addition to that, her shame left her feeling that she needed punishment and who better to meet those needs than the sure thing! She was with a man that was going to beat her regularly and meet her shame needs of punishment.

It wouldn't have mattered if she would have gotten out of her current relationship; she would have just been attracted to another sick man, because that's all she could see. I could have lined 50 men up and down the hallway, 49 of whom were relatively healthy and one of whom was an abusive outlaw and let her look them all over. Guess which one she would be attracted to? Guess which one she would go home with? That's right, the outlaw. Her shame had turned her into a "sick magnet". Sick men and predators are able to spot this vulnerability from shame a mile away. They know they will not be rejected, because the young woman barely believes she has the right to breathe air, let alone say "no" to anyone about anything they want to do to her. These unhealthy men are like coyotes lurking on the edge of a pasture salivating over a wounded calf.

If a shame-filled person can't find somebody else to punish them, they will oftentimes do it themselves. I have sadly watched it happen many times over the years. A man begins a program of recovery and starts living better and feeling better. He finds a new job, starts a new relationship, saves a little money and begins to become physically healthier. But then he pulls the whole structure down around his ears because he knows he is not worthy of all these good things. He sabotages his own success, because he fears that if he elevates his life any higher, it is really going to hurt when he falls from that height, and of course, it is inevitable in his mind that he will fall.

Whenever a recovering addict keeps relapsing after experiencing some success, you can bet the farm that they have unresolved shame issues. The garbage that is underneath their current success will eventually seep up and spoil everything they have been working on. The dark secrets of past damage from others will prevent any lasting healing.

So, if that is true (and it is), then what is the cure for shame? The cure for shame is exposure. Those dark secrets must be dragged out into the light, looked at and then discarded. The fear of a shame-filled person is that if anybody ever found out what happened to them, they would feel dirtier and less loveable than they already do. Shame binds itself to more shame by keeping the secrets. That is why children rarely share any sexual abuse with their parents or guardians. They are afraid that they will be viewed as so dirty and bad that they will be unlovable and losing that love would be devastating.

I have used the following true story to help patients understand what makes shame grow and what can destroy toxic shame. Some years ago I was visiting relatives in western Pennsylvania. They have any number of abandoned coal mines in that area and they use some of them in an interesting way. They have discovered that mushrooms will grow really well in the dark, dank mine shafts, so that's what they use them for. The Campbell's Soup Company and other companies have flats of mushroom trays down in the mines. They buy rotten hay and manure from the local farmers and put that on the flats of mushrooms and man, can they grow mushrooms down there.

However, if they scrape the hay and manure off these mushrooms and bring them up out of the mine and into the sunlight, in about 3 days they will be dead. Shame is like mushrooms. If you keep it in the dark and feed it crap it will really grow, but if you drag it out into the light and scrape the crap off it, it will die.

Once the shame is exposed, then it can be examined and the shaming messages can be evaluated to see if the person really is as bad as they feel or if the messages just came from sick people doing sick things to them. When shameful behavior happens to children, they always believe that it must be their fault, because their prefrontal brain development is not at the point where they can see any issue from any perspective but their own. They do not have the capacity to see things from another's perspective and their thinking is all egocentric.

Here is an example of this egocentric thinking. I was playing hide-and-seek with my young grandsons in the house one rainy day. One of the boys thought he was hidden, because his face and torso were behind the big chair, but his whole rear end and legs were sticking out. Because he could not see me, he thought that I couldn't see him. He just could not envision another perspective at that time in his brain development.

Another example is that I asked this child's twin brother a question about the sky as we were looking up at the clouds, imagining different animals from the shape of the clouds. Just to see what he would say, I asked him, "Tyler, why is the sky blue"? Without hesitating he responded, "Because blue is my favorite color". Again, it is all about him and all from his perspective.

The really damaging aspect of this for children is that if there is tension in a home, the children will pick up on it first and will believe it is their fault. The kids and the family pets will feel the tension first, because that's all they have to go on is their feelings. Their thought processes aren't developed enough to think something like, "Well, it appears that my mother and father have a difference of opinion about a financial issue and they are angry with one another, but fortunately, that has nothing to do with me". Nope, if there is anger the kids and pets will feel it. The kids will believe they are the cause of the problem and the pets will cower under the end table. They are both being shamed by the adult's shameful behavior. When adults act shamelessly, children and pets are shamed.

Children may not be able to understand these shame experiences when they are young and they will be damaged by them. However, later on as adults, there is an opportunity to look at these messages and decide whether they were based on anything real or true and if not, then they can be disregarded.

Another example that I have used to great effect in group therapy is to tell them the following true story. My uncle, Ervin was a gunner on a B-17 in World War II. He had some Post-Traumatic Stress Disorder symptoms when he came back from the war. He liked to do quiet things like work in his rose garden after the war. One other enterprise that he started was to buy and refurbish antiques. He was into antiques before it was really cool. He used to go to farm auctions and buy old furniture that he thought might have some value and fix it up. One time the auctioneer had moved over to the machine shed and was selling a box of tools that was sitting on a little table. He said he would bundle the whole thing together and throw in the table with the tools. Uncle Ervin bought everything for $15.00.

The table was all covered with oil cans, hay and sparrow droppings. It had been painted over many different times. It had 3 legs and was round on one side and flat on the other. It had glass balls held on by brass claws for the feet, but these were mostly obscured by dirt and oil. Uncle Ervin took that table and began working on it. He cleaned it off, glued the joints and stripped the paint off layer by layer until he was down to the bare wood. To his surprise, he found that it was made of beautiful black walnut wood. He cleaned the brass claws and glass ball feet as well. He refinished the wood with a beautiful stain and varnished it.

The amazing thing was that not only was this little table a beautiful piece, once all the crap was cleared off it, but he looked it up in an antique catalogue and found out that it was a very rare piece. He ended up selling that table for fifteen hundred dollars!

At the end of telling this story I ask the patient what this has to do with him or her. They usually see themselves in the story and answer something like, "I'm that little table aren't I"? "Yes you are", I respond. "Somebody treated that little table as if it were worthless and threw it out in the shed and put oil cans on it and let the sparrows crap on it. But was there anything wrong with the table or was there just something wrong with the people who were too dumb or too sick to recognize its value?" "It was them and not me", the patient responded.

The difficult, but possible recovery from toxic shame can happen when a person looks at the shaming messages and events from an adult perspective and evaluates each one and throws out the ones that are based on sickness and lies. When a patient can say, "It was them and not me", they are on their way to recovery.

7

Anger

Another emotion that keeps the feelings disease of addiction going is anger. Addicts discover relatively quickly that one way to keep other people off their backs about their using is to react in very hostile, angry and ornery ways. Family members and friends begin to be gradually trained to not say anything about drinking, using drugs, gambling or anything else, because when they do it gets very nasty around the house. People in the family talk about other things as if they are important and keep silent about the very thing that is tearing their family apart. If you have ever heard the phrase, "The elephant in the living room", you can be sure that this phrase got started with family members talking all around the issue of addiction, but never mentioning addiction.

The other thing that anger does is to keep the addict from feeling other feelings that could lead to honesty and surrender. Anger covers hurt and hurt covers fear. That is why if you are observing a man who is acting very angry much of the time, you can be sure that he is a man who has a lot of sadness and/or a lot of fear. All addicts are very afraid to get to the more vulnerable feelings that lurk underneath anger, namely, hurt and fear.

Other people who are not addicted do the same thing, but not nearly so often or so vehemently. For example, I attended a cookout at some friends of ours some years ago. The children were playing with a beach ball in the front yard and were kicking it high in the air and catching it. Some of the little children joined in the game and were having a great time. But then one of the teenagers thumped that beach ball way up in the air and it soared out over the street. A little four year old boy went peeling out after the ball and went into the street. At that same time, a car full of teens came around the corner and down that street. The child's mother was standing on the porch, looking on in horror as her child and the car were converging. The car screeched to a halt and stopped just in time that it did not really strike the child, but did tip him over. The mother came running off the porch, screaming at her child and swearing at the teenagers in the car. She picked that child up and swatted his behind so hard that he cried for ten minutes.

That mother reacted with anger, but really what she was feeling was fear. She was scared to death that she was going to watch her child get run over and killed, but what she displayed was anger. Why? Because anger gets us mobilized and ready for action better than does fear and because we feel less vulnerable with anger than we do with hurt or fear.

An example of how anger covers hurt happened to a classmate of mine when we were in college. He had been through a rather turbulent relationship with his girlfriend for several months. He was very obsessed with her, but did not always do things to make her feel very secure in the relationship. One day she finally had enough and told him that she just couldn't go on with the relationship anymore and they needed to break up.

That guy was so teed off that he had almost nothing left in his dorm room that wasn't broken after his tirade. He called that girl everything but a Christian and swore a blue streak about how she had dumped him and what terrible things he wanted to do to her.

He was acting so angry. It was not the time for me to say anything then, because he would have probably turned that anger on me and he was pretty out of control. But I wondered inside my own head why he was acting so angry. Why wasn't he expressing sadness? After all, this gal was supposedly the love of his life. Why wasn't he sorry to lose her? The appropriate feelings should have been sorrow, sadness, loneliness and grief, but that is not what he was displaying. Not surprisingly, this young man went on to become an alcoholic as the years went on.

If you can picture the physical stance that a person has when feeling the different emotions, you can see why folks choose anger instead of other feelings. The anger pose has us with feet apart, fists raised, blood pumping into our face and neck and eyes blazing. This pose puts us in a very well-defended position.

Being in the sad pose has us looking down with our hands at our sides, shoulders slumped and possibly even tears streaming down our faces. This is a much more vulnerable position than anger.

The fear pose would show us with our backs against the wall, with arms outspread, eyes rolling back in our heads and our mouths hanging open. This is the most vulnerable position of all the emotions and has the highest chance of us getting destroyed in some way.

The danger, from an addicted person's viewpoint, is that if they ever get beneath the anger, they will have to deal with not only hurt and fear, but other things like guilt and shame and grief and loss. If they would ever have to face these feelings, they might have to quit using the addictive agents and what addict wants to do that? Anger protects the addiction and enables it to continue.

One way to picture the process of what feelings might be appropriate to feel, but then what feelings are acted out in behavior is to picture an addicted person like a huge funnel. All kinds of emotions go into the top of the funnel: sadness, irritation, pleasure, fear, boredom and loneliness. But when all these feelings come out the bottom of the funnel in terms of reaction and behavior, they all look like anger, because anger leaves us the best defended.

So far, we have been talking about active anger and it is the most common kind, but it is certainly not the only kind. The active anger does seem to shut other people up most effectively, but there are other ways to be angry. A person doesn't have to start yelling, threaten physical violence, curse, swear or start breaking things to get the point across that bringing up the drinking, using or other addictive behavior is just not something that we do here.

Passive anger can work to keep others from mentioning "the elephant in the living room" as well. Passive anger is not about what you do to another person; it is about what you don't do with them. The most common form of passive anger is one that most folks who are married know something about, namely, the silent treatment. Spouses are sometimes punished by the cold silence of their partner when they brush by them and will not even respond to direct questions. There is hostility to this kind of silence that is unmistakable.

Here is a tip for all the men out there who have faced some passive anger from their wives or girlfriends. You might feel the chill in the room as your woman brusquely walks past you without speaking or even looking at you. You sense that you must have done something wrong, but can't for the life of you figure out what it might be. Don't be fooled when you ask, "What's wrong"? When she says, "Nothing" with a rise in pitch on the second syllable of that word, don't believe her. It is never "nothing" and you are going to have to do some detective work to find out just exactly how you managed to step in it or it is just going to keep getting colder in that room.

Another way to use passive anger to control others is to withhold affection from them. We are again punishing people not by what we are doing to them, but by what we are not doing with them. For example, we might not kiss our family members hello when we come into the house. We might go in the other room and not join the family watching television in the living room. We might not give the kids hugs and kisses before bed. We might refuse to have sex with our partner. We might give no attention or eye contact when our friend speaks to us and might just keep staring at our Smart Phone. Anybody can use passive anger to control, but addicted persons use it regularly.

Yet another aspect of using anger to control is the use of sarcasm. Most people don't think of sarcasm as being anger, but it is. Sarcasm is really sideways anger. It is anger that is thinly veiled with humor attached to it. It is anger that can be directed at another person, but if they call you on it, you can always back away from what you said by saying, "Just kidding". I refer to sarcasm as "chicken crap anger", because using it always leaves you a back door to slip out of if somebody else calls your bluff and tells you something hurts or is mean-spirited.

An example of this is a conversation I had with an acquaintance many years ago when I was in training to become an addiction counselor. This man asked me what I was doing now, since he hadn't seen me for some years. I told him that I had finished my chaplaincy training and was now doing my internship to become an addiction counselor. I told him that I was excited about working with addictions and I thought it was a line of work that suited me well.

His response was to say, "So, you finally found something you can do, huh"? I was caught either way I went concerning this statement. If I just said nothing and took it, he had jabbed me pretty good. However, if I would have said something about the fact that it wasn't like my life had been one big failure up to that point, he would have responded that he was just kidding and wasn't it a shame that with all this education, I had lost my sense of humor. Sarcasm is a way of gouging people without having to be responsible or take ownership for doing it. You can always tell if what you are experiencing is good-natured humor or controlling sarcasm, because the jabs from sarcasm always take flesh out with it when the harpoon is pulled out, whereas humor does not take flesh with it.

Although these are all types of anger that addicted people use, there is another form of anger that is even more popular and more damaging and that is resentment. Resentment is just anger that we have been sitting on for a long time. Resentment builds easily in addicted persons, because whenever another person does something to them that hurts, they don't deal with it immediately and appropriately - they drink or use another addictive agent and push that resentment deeper inside themselves. These resentments build up until there is an explosion.

Holding onto resentments is like walking out into a field on the farm with a big burlap bag to pick up rocks so they won't ruin your machinery. You pick up one rock and throw it in the sack and that's fine. But then you pick up another and another and another and pretty soon that sack is heavy. Then, without warning, the bottom of the sack breaks and all those rocks land on your toes. There needs to be a way to deal with one rock at a time and not let them build up.

Another example for resentments comes from the farm. When I was growing up we had bantam hens running around loose on the farm. They oftentimes made nests in holes in the straw in the barn. They would lay as many as two dozen eggs at times, but they couldn't always get back to the nest, because straw would be moved and it would prevent them from returning. By the time they were able to sit on those eggs, they were rotten and would never hatch anything. But those hens just kept going back and sitting on those rotten eggs. In a similar way, addicted persons often sit on their resentments for years, but nothing good is ever going to be hatched from this. They are rotten and might as well be discarded.

The Big Book of Alcoholics Anonymous is very clear that addicts cannot hold resentments and stay sober. It states, "Resentment is the number one offender. It kills more alcoholics than anything else". It goes on to talk about how spiritually damaging sitting on this anger is and that a recovering person must be free of this kind of anger. When the behavior of others is allowed to disturb one's serenity, relapse is already happening and if left unchecked will lead to using again and destruction.

One of the difficult, but necessary tasks of recovery is for addicts to find a way to let go of resentments and forgive other people. It is a difficult thing for all of us, with or without addictions. Most of us only get as far as recognizing that other people have wronged us and that's as far as we get. The result is that others continue to wrong us and we feel resentful and believe that we should be able to recriminate against them and get even somehow. We tell ourselves that unless we receive justice, we can never move on and experience any peace and serenity.

It is also a lot easier to see how other people have hurt us than it is to see how we might have hurt other people. This is especially true for addicted people. The denial and delusion oftentimes leads to ridiculous differences in looking at the flaws of others from the flaws in oneself.

I remember one patient in drug/alcohol treatment that was seething with rage and resentment because of what he said that his wife had done that really hurt him. He said that he had come home one day from work and had completely cleaned out the whole garage and put things neatly back. He was livid because his wife had not given him one compliment on this. She also had embarrassed him in front of his friends by telling him that he needed to quit drinking beer and get home on one occasion. The way he talked, one would think that these were hanging offenses that his wife had committed.

However, when his family week rolled around, we began to find out a much different story. This was a man that had spent all their family vacation money on building a bar in their basement, had cheated on his wife and was forgiven, had missed most of the kids sporting events, and had called his wife a bitch in front of his drinking buddies. The amazing thing is that when all this came out in family group, he still didn't think that his mistakes were as great as hers were!

So, part of the problem in recovery is to be able to see clearly what our own mistakes have really been and how deeply they have hurt other people before looking at how others have hurt us. Getting a realistic picture of the comparison of mistakes and hurts is part of getting honest.

The other part of recovery is to be willing to let go of hurt and resentments even if the other person really did do a lot worse to us than we did to them. This is where forgiveness comes in.

Forgiveness is not reserved for after such a time as the other person who has wronged us apologizes or makes up for what they have done. If we wait for the other person to get what they deserve, that isn't forgiveness – it is justice. Justice means that I get what I deserve and the other fellow gets what he deserves. Forgiveness is much different from that. When I forgive, I give the other fellow what he doesn't deserve, for good. I set aside the penalty for what the other has done and let it go. But, you might say, that doesn't sound fair! It's not fair. Forgiveness is never fair, but it is cleansing and it is healthy.

If I am an addicted person, what I am trying to do with forgiveness is to stop letting other people from living in my head rent-free. Forgiveness is then a gift that I am giving to myself to be free from carrying around all the rocks of resentment we talked about earlier. If an addict wants to live, he or she must be free of resentment or it kills them. This business of resentment is infinitely grave and fatal.

8

Fear

If you want to get down to the level where people really live, you have to get to the fears. It is our fears that hold us back from being the kind of people we could be. It is our fears that prevent us from taking risks. It is also our fears that lead us to want to find something that will allay these fears and hold them at bay. Not surprisingly, what many folks find to numb these fears is the same thing they find to numb other feelings, namely, addictive agents.

There are numerous fears that we can have and all of them are worth talking about, because they play into addictions so heavily. One of the most important fears is the fear of rejection. There is a part of all of us that would like to feel accepted. We all want to be thought well of and appreciated. It is true that there are many people who would try to tell you that they don't care what anybody else thinks about them, but that just isn't true. They may act like they don't care what anybody else thinks about them, but unless they are a total sociopath, they do care.

We know that being accepted and cared for is a basic human need. If we are not loved and accepted and cared for as infants we will most likely have a failure to thrive. I remember reading about an experiment that was done many decades ago with babies in an orphanage. All of the babies were given their basic physical needs, such as: milk and food, changed diapers, baths, medications, etc. Half of these babies not only had these physical needs met but also had emotional needs of acceptance met as well. These babies were picked up and held. They were talked to and fussed over. They were touched, stroked and kissed.

The result of the experiment was that after a year of this differing care, the babies that got the extra emotional care were almost all thriving and healthy. The half that only had physical needs met did not do so well at all. In fact, almost half of those babies had died. They were all raised in the same big room, so it was not like a disease or plague had affected one half of the room. These babies got the ultimate shaming message when they were not accepted and that message was "I shouldn't exist" and so they did not.

This is a terrible experiment and will not be repeated for obvious reasons, but it does very forcefully demonstrate the need for acceptance and why people fear rejection so deeply.

As we move from infants to young children there are many situations that can lead to rejection. For example, children are always crushed when they are not included for games and activities. I recall a process when I was young called "choosing up sides". Two kids would be captains and they would choose back and forth which players they wanted until nobody was left. The real issue was that nobody wanted to be the last player picked, because that meant rejection. You were pretty much viewed as a throw-in liability to your team.

Then there was the anxiety over who was going to get invited to the birthday parties and who was going to get left out. Not every party included everybody in your grade. Some parties made it a very exclusive thing and it was clear who rated and who didn't. There was even some one-ups-man-ship on who brought the best and most expensive present.

I recall that the practice of giving nicknames was prevalent in grade school. It seemed that the popular kids didn't have much for nicknames, but the kids who were marginal had lots of them and they weren't very complimentary either. The names like "stinky", "gooney bird", "cricket", "goofball" and "horse face" are probably still burned in the brain of some unfortunate classmates.

As I look back on my own grade school experiences, it is clear to me that the kids who were picked on and given the uncomplimentary nicknames were being shamed mercilessly. But the thing that I didn't see at that time, but now see clearly, is that the kids who were picking on others were kids who came from dysfunctional homes where there were lots of shaming things going on. These kids were trying to dump off the shame that they got in their home onto some other poor schmucks if they would take it. There were certain kids that got blamed for everything. I can remember the chant of "Randy did it, Randy did it" as poor Randy got the business by all of us. I can also remember scrambling just as fast as everyone else to make sure I did not become Randy.

Those kids who were fortunate enough to come from loving, functional homes did not usually pile on when certain kids were being shamed, because they didn't have much shame to get rid of and didn't need to find a scapegoat.

When we reach adolescence the fear of rejection and need for acceptance becomes as strong as it will ever be. In fact, if you were to ask me what I believe the greatest need is for an adolescent, I would say that it is the need to belong, to fit in, to be accepted and be included.

Adolescents are willing to do crazy and dangerous things just to be accepted. All you need to do to realize this is look at some of the clothing that teenagers will wear. There are styles that do very little to enhance the appearance of a young man or young woman, but they will all wear them. Why? It was because all the other young folks are wearing them.

I think back to when my son was about 14 years old. He was wearing some basketball shorts that looked about three sizes too big for him. The back of them would swish around when he ran and it looked as if he had pooped his pants. I told him about that, which he greatly appreciated by saying, "Oh, Dad, you don't know anything about this". But then later on in the day his buddies Billy and Joey came over to play basketball in our driveway and I noticed that it looked like they had filled their britches also! I saw the need to fit in at work here again.

I have also been intrigued by certain hairstyles that teenagers will display. My favorite is the style where one side of the head is shaved and the other side is long and drapes down over one eye in front, effectively rendering the person blind in that one eye. Sometimes it can be streaked with green, red and blue color also, which makes it even more appealing, apparently. While I might see this as bordering on the ridiculous, teens might see it as a real expression of individuality and the wearer of that style might gain some acceptance for having it.

I once commented on all of my son's friends wearing their pants all hanging off their rear ends and I was informed by my son that this kid was just being an individual. "Do you mean being an individual like all the other kids who are doing exactly the same thing", I responded? "Oh Dad, you don't know", my son retorted.

While wearing weird clothing and hairstyles may be harmless, there are plenty of other things that teens do that can be quite dangerous. Driving way too fast for conditions, jumping off roofs, letting somebody punch you in the face or holding onto fireworks in your bare hands are all ways to prove that you are tough and cool and therefore, acceptable.

I can recall climbing up into the silo on the farm when I was a teen and walking across the plank with nothing underneath me. We used to sneak up on sleeping steers in the feedlot and climb on them and get bucked off just to see if we could do it. We stood up on bicycles, climbed up ropes and jumped out of the haymow as a way of accepting challenges from the neighbor kids. Taking dares and doing dangerous and foolish things is not something that is new for kids now. This has gone on for a long time.

But by far, the easiest way to avoid rejection and gain acceptance for today's young people is to simply be part of a group that is drinking, using drugs or is using some other addictive agent. There is automatic acceptance when a bunch of kids are sitting and passing a joint around between them. There is a feeling of comradeship as the joint or the bottle is passed from one to the other. There is a bond that is being formed, not just because all are doing the same thing, but because all are engaging in a handy form of rebellion, since all are doing an illegal thing together.

In addition, if someone's behavior gets nasty or beyond the bounds of appropriateness when drinking or using, the person can always just say that they were drunk or high and the whole episode is written off and excused. There is no rejection for inappropriate behavior when using, so a person can take the risk of doing or saying things that they would normally be too inhibited from doing or saying and if it doesn't work out well, they can just say, "Well, I was pretty drunk".

After working with several addicted coeds from the local university, I have come to understand that the mating call of a college girl is the following: "I am so wasted"! Drinking and using drugs is viewed as an appropriate reason for irresponsible sexual behavior in the college setting. The fear of rejection is alleviated by chemical usage.

There are many other fears besides the fear of rejection that addictive agents are used to cover up. Fear of failure is another prominent fear. Addicted or not, we all have a fear of not being successful at something. But sometimes it is more than not just having success, but the thought of looking really stupid if we try something and fail. Most of us have potential to do many things and even great things, but we don't try them, because we are afraid of looking bad or stupid. We stick to the safe things that we know to avoid that sense of failure that might occur if we try something new. For example, I don't care much for mechanics or fixing things on machinery and only do what I know. But I think my disinterest really stems from a fear that I will fail if I try to fix some things, so it is just better to say that I am not interested. I believe it goes all the way back to when I was a kid and my uncle would tease me if I couldn't seem to figure something out and fix it on the farm. Probably the reason I am a chaplain and addiction counselor instead of a farmer or rancher is because I didn't want to fail at it because of all the machinery fixing there is on a farm. Ranching is better than farming, because there is not as much machinery to fix. This probably explains why I have beef cows, but no crops today on my acreage.

Another example that I have seen of this fear is in the area of singing. I enjoy singing and have been in several choirs, musicals and singing groups. But I run into people all the time that tell me that they can't sing and are tone deaf. My wife tells me that she can't sing, but I have heard her singing to the radio in the car and singing around the house when she thinks that I am not around. She is not bad and can carry a tune if she tries, but she rarely tries when other people can hear her, because she is afraid to sound bad and fail. Very few people are actually tone deaf - they just lack confidence in singing and fear failure.

There are times when people are put in situations where they believe they will fail and so they let others know by their words or by their actions that they are not really trying. I remember having to be in a footrace with a kid in the class ahead of me that was really a good runner. I wasn't that bad at running, but I knew that he would beat me, so I made an elaborate show that I wasn't really trying in the race, as if to say that the race really didn't count, because I wasn't trying. The reality was that I just didn't want to lose and be seen as a failure by my schoolmates.

Another fear that is oftentimes covered by chemical usage is the fear of intimacy. It is a fearful thing to know and be truly known by another. Intimacy requires not only time, but risk. As long as I can save parts of myself from being known by another, they cannot really reject me, because they don't know the real me or the whole me. They may be viewing the cardboard cutout figure of me that I present to the world, but they don't know the real me behind that figure, so they can't wound the real me.

This fear ties into our previous discussion of shame. If a person has been abused in some way and feels bad, dirty, worthless and unlovable, it is very difficult to be honest and share what has happened for fear that the other person will think that I am even worse than I already feel. That is why it takes real courage to expose the shameful things that have happened and gain trust and achieve intimacy.

Many times addicts mistake sex for intimacy and believe that if they have had sex with another person, that they have been intimate. That is not true. You can have sex without intimacy, but by the same token, you can also have intimacy without sex. There are people who have become great friends and have shared their inmost thoughts and secrets with each other, but have never had sex with them. On the other hand, there are people who have been obsessed with sex, sex and more sex, but have never really been intimate with anyone. They have taken no risks in sharing and have only shared their bodies, but not their souls.

Fear of death is another powerful fear and in our culture, talking about death is not seen as an appropriate topic. The denial of death is very pervasive in this culture. People don't even say the word, "dead" or "death". At the hospital we have patients that die almost every day and chaplains are called at every death to see if we can give some spiritual or emotional comfort. Most of the time family members of the deceased don't say that their loved one has died; they say that he or she has "passed". That is a much more antiseptic and soft word to use in place of "dead". If somebody is going to have serious surgery, their family members don't talk about the fear of death, but rather say things like, "What if he doesn't make it", or "What if this doesn't turn out"?

It is almost as if we can bring about death by talking about it directly. As long as nobody mentions the possibility that death could occur in this hospitalization, then it can't happen. I once got written up by a family member of a patient and had to talk to my supervisor, because I mentioned death in a prayer. The situation was that a 40 year-old man was critically ill. He had several disabilities and had some kind of disease that people usually didn't survive very long. Actually, he had lived a few years already beyond the usual expectation. I had a prayer with the comatose patient and his father one day and then came back the next day when the patient's sister was also there. This was a family with Christian background, so I felt I was on solid ground in talking about being with the Lord in this life and in the life beyond after death. But apparently, I wasn't supposed to say anything about death. The sister turned on me like a rabid dog and told me that she never wanted me to come back again and pray negatively over her brother. She said, "He should only be hearing positive things like he is going to get better and he is going to be alright and he is going to go back home and be o.k."

The fact that the patient was in a coma and may not have been able to hear me made no difference to her. The fact that his vital signs were very bad and he looked like he was dying made no difference either. In her eyes I had prayed negatively by mentioning the word, death. The end of the story is that the patient died 2 days later. But I am sure that his sister believed that the reason he didn't pull out of that disease is because of the negative praying of that damnable negative chaplain!

Addicted persons are very sensitive to any talk about death and greatly fear death. There is something that really eats away at an addicted person when somebody mentions that if they don't quit using, they could die. That is the thought they have been trying to keep out of their heads and when people keep bringing it up, it is very annoying. But deep down inside of addicts is the knowledge that it is not like their using might kill them; it is already killing them! It is just a question of how much time before the death comes. It might not be sudden as from an overdose or a car accident. It might be a slow, lingering death from emphysema, cirrhosis, heart failure or stroke. But there will be death; that is a certainty, without recovery. In Alcoholics Anonymous meetings people are reminded that besides recovery the only other options for an addict are death, imprisonment or insanity and sometimes addicts experience all three from their disease.

Of all the fears human beings can have, one of the greatest fears is the fear of the unknown. This is a particularly difficult fear for addicted people. They know what it is like to feel drunk and hung over. They know what it is like to be dope sick with withdrawal from opiates and desperate to get a fix that will help them to get well. They know what it is like to feel guilt-ridden and wondering what they actually did the night before. What they don't know is what it might be like to try to live without drugs, alcohol, gambling, sex, video games or whatever else their addiction might be.

The questions that come to mind are endless when considering this possibility. What would I do to relax? What would I do if I couldn't sit around with my buddies and pass a joint around? Where would I go for fun if I couldn't go to the bar? Who would I have for friends if I am not going to use with them? How would I face scary situations without a little buzz on? How would I ever have any fun? Would I just be sitting around twiddling my thumbs and saying, "Oh boy, I'm sober, this is totally boring".

So, even though an addict knows all the pain that addiction brings, they don't have any idea what being clean and sober might be and fear that it might be worse.

Here is a farm example of fear of the unknown. We had a cow

that died after giving birth to a red and white speckled calf that we ingeniously named Speckle. We bottle-fed Speckle in the front box stall of the barn, which was rather dark and dank, because that part of the barn was underground. As the months went by, Speckle grew and got to the size that we could turn her out in the feedlot with the other feeder cattle. It was a beautiful day in May and the cattle had eaten their fill and were lounging out in the sunshine, having a great day. We opened the gate to Speckle's stall and had to drive her out of her pen. She walked down the alleyway and got to the doorway that led to the outside. The sunlight was cutting across the doorway, making a clear line of demarcation between the dark inside of the barn and the brilliant outside. Speckle stood with her nose almost, but not quite touching the light, but would not go outside. Her whole hide shook as she stood there, then she walked back into the interior darkness. She came towards the light again, but shook and would not go out. It took her 20 minutes to finally step out into the light. After she did, she found that it was alright and began jumping up and down, spinning around and head-butting the other cattle.

What Speckle demonstrated very clearly was that the fear of the unknown is oftentimes more powerful than the pain of that which we get used to. Even though her pen was in the dark and she had been all alone, still, she knew what to expect there. But the great outdoors was a whole new thing and it was scary.

We can see the same thing in ourselves as humans. We do something that doesn't work very well and may even hurt us and then when it doesn't work, we do the same thing over again, only harder. It may not work and it may hurt, but at least we know what to expect. My colleague, Jim used to always say concerning this aspect of human nature, "You know, we don't make many mistakes in life - we just make the same ones over and over again"!

That is what makes change of any kind so difficult, this fear of the unknown. I read a story recently about a man who was on vacation in Kentucky and he was lost. He stopped at a shack that had an old fellow sitting on his porch, smoking a corn-cob pipe. His blue tick hound was lying on the porch next to him. As he was getting directions from the old hillbilly, every once in a while the hound would raise up a little and let out a mournful howl as only a hound can do. The man finally asked the old-timer what was wrong with his dog. The old fellow said, "Oh, he's lying on a nail that is sticking up out of the boards". "Well, why doesn't he move", the man asked? "Well, it's not really hurting him bad enough to do anything about it", the owner replied. "he just likes to bitch about it once in a while".

That is kind of who we are as people too. Things may not be bad enough to move or do anything different and our fear of the unknown kicks in, but we do like to bitch about it once in a while.

If we want to overcome this fear there are some things that it might be helpful to remember. In the first place, 90% of what we fear will never happen. We spend an awful lot of time anticipating things that will never take place. It would be a much better use of our time to not fret over the 90% that won't happen and just wait until the other 10% does happen and then deal with that. I read an acronym once on dealing with fear that said the letters, F-E-A-R stand for "False Evidence Appearing Real". In other words, we can dream up all kinds of things that aren't really there and then obsess on that.

Another thing that I have discovered that works for me is to remember the phrase, "Action conquers fear". Whenever I am apprehensive about some situation, if I simply take the first step and do some kind of action, the fear lessens. For example, when I was challenged to write this book, I had several fears: how would I find the time, would it be something that anybody would want to read and how should it all be organized. But what I found is that when I simply decided to sit down and write out my outline, then the fears went away and the excitement of a new project took over.

Similarly, when an addicted person faces the fear of the unknown about what a life of sobriety would be like and what they might have to do to begin this life, it is action that will conquer fear. I remember a patient that I had worked with that said he just didn't know if these A.A. meetings would be for him or if people there could understand his particular situation. He had all kinds of projected thoughts of what might happen to him and how this fellowship might not fit him and how it seemed like a big commitment of time, etc. Finally, his new sponsor solved the problem of the fears for him by simply telling him, "Just get your ass to the meetings. Your head will show up later"! Action conquers fear again.

9
Grief and Loss

Of the many feelings that people use addictive substances to cope with, grief and loss are two of the most common. Whenever we lose something or someone that is important to us, it causes intense pain as well as fear. We experience the pain of loss and the fear that we will not be able to go on in life without that person or that thing that meant so much to us. When that happens, people oftentimes reach for something that will dull the pain and then keep using that agent until they become dependent on it.

I hear the stories almost every week in group therapy on the psychiatric unit about how patients started using mood-altering substances to cope with losses. In fact, there were four addicts in a recent group of patients and three of them told the story of how loss began their downward slide into dependency. One man said that his mother died two years ago and he went to the Dr. and got some Fentanyl to help him through the grieving. But he kept on using this pain-killer after the acute grieving period and became dependent on it. He was not really a drinker or user before this time and is extremely embarrassed now at having lost control of this substance.

Another woman in the group lost her mother about 6 years ago and started taking some Xanax to calm her down. Then last year she lost her husband and six months later her son committed suicide. Her using has skyrocketed since that time and she knows now that she is hooked and needs help.

The third person in the group was a young woman that lost both of her parents in a motor vehicle accident 5 years ago and last year lost her best friend to suicide. She has been drinking alcohol and using heroin ever since these losses.

All of these patients found out that using addictive substances is not a very healthy or effective way to deal with grief and loss even though it provided some temporary relief at first. As we said before, people start using to solve problems and then find out that it doesn't work very long and then in fact, starts causing more problems. The solution has become the problem.

Using chemicals to deal with loss is a little like something that old-timers in Minnesota say about dealing with frostbite in the winter. They would advise that one put his hand in snow and the frostbite would not hurt. While that is true, it is the exact wrong thing to do. The tissue should be warmed up as quickly as possible. Even lukewarm water will burn like fire at first, but that is what needs to happen. Likewise in grieving we need to feel our feelings of loss even if it burns at first.

There are many losses that we might incur in life, all the way from major losses, such as people dying that we love, to small everyday losses. When we talk about grief and loss the only thing people usually think about is death. When we lose someone close to us, we believe that we are grieving and we are, but that is by far, not the extent of our losses in life.

Let's look at some common losses, some of which are huge, some of which are small and some of which are in between. We know that the death of a loved one tops the list. Divorce is another common, but painful loss. Getting an abortion is a huge loss, even if it looks like the best option at the time. The loss of a relationship, such as a friendship, boyfriend or girlfriend can be very painful. Imprisonment is a tremendous loss of freedom and dignity. Losing your home through fire, flood or repossession is traumatic. The aging process means that we incur a lot of losses, such as: loss of hair, teeth, flexibility and energy. Losing a pet is surprisingly, one of the most common losses that people have a hard time overcoming. I know people that would rather lose one of their family members than lose their dog. The loss of a promotion at work can be very disappointing. Even something like losing your wallet can be a real hassle with the need to cancel credit cards, get a new driver's license and replace identification. There are football fans that have to grieve after their team loses, which seems silly only to those people who are not obsessed with football.

Some of these losses certainly will strike you as greater and some as lesser, but that varies depending upon the person. The significance of any loss depends on two things: the intensity of our attachment to that person or thing and how much the loss disrupts our daily habits and routines. Having said that, now I want to consider one loss that we did not list above, but is at the very heart of our discussion, namely, recovery from addiction.

The loss of an addicted person's best buddy, booze and drugs or other addictive agents, is a huge loss, probably exceeded only by death. When we think of our criteria for how significant a loss is in our lives, we must first consider the intensity of our attachment to that person or thing. This is fairly obvious. Addicted persons are so attached to their drug or other addictive agent that they will "pursue it to the gates of hell or insanity". There is nothing too low or depraved that can be done if it will ensure that an addict can keep on using. There is nothing that will not be done if it enables one to keep the game going of using. Addiction is a mental obsession that can be combined with a physical compulsion and that certainly shows the attachment that exists to the addictive agent.

The other criteria that shows the significance of a loss is how much the loss of that thing interrupts our daily routine. With addiction this is also very strong. Addicts in treatment often feel lost as to what they are going to do if they are not using anymore. They ask questions like: "What am I going to do for fun from now on? Who am I going to do it with? Where can I go if I can't go to the bar or to parties? What am I going to have to help me relax? What if I get hurt and have pain – then what am I going to do?"

These are all important questions and people must struggle through them without any anesthesia to find the answers. What they soon realize is that recovery from addiction is really one giant grief and loss process and the sooner they learn how to grieve well, the sooner their life will again have meaning and the light at the end of the tunnel will not just be the train coming to run them over.

Actually, when you think about it, one way to look at life is that it is just one long series of losses. It starts the moment we leave our mother's womb and continues until the ultimate loss on the day that we die. When we are born, we leave the safe, warm, wet water world in which we have dwelt for nine months and come out into the harsh light of a hospital room (in most cases) and people immediately start doing invasive things to us like suctioning things out of us, clipping things off us and washing stuff off us. We are already experiencing loss and that just continues throughout life in the large and small losses we talked about earlier.

So, if that is true (and it is), then we could say that the quality of any person's life will hinge directly on how well they learn to grieve losses. It is not like there are some people who have losses and other people who don't. Everybody experiences loss. Some may seem to have more than their share, but we all do feel loss many times throughout our lives. So, you can't divide the world up into the folks who never have any losses, who would be known as the "happy people" and those who have losses, who would be called the "sad people". It doesn't split up along those lines. There are folks who have had the most gosh awful things happen to them in their lives and yet are still people who find joy, are positive and find life meaningful. On the other hand, there are people who have not really had it that bad when it comes to major losses in life and yet are negative, selfish and miserable. The difference is that the happy group has learned how to grieve well and the sad group has not.

It is not an easy thing to learn to grieve well, because grief affects us in all aspects of being human. Grief affects us physically. People who are grieving heavily will oftentimes get physically sick. The stress of a major loss will release hormones like cortisol in our body, which can be useful in that it gets us ready for either fight or flight, but is damaging in that it lowers our resistance to disease. Illnesses that our immune system would normally throw off, become things that we succumb to under the stress of loss. What we normally see is that about two months after a particularly trying time or time of loss, we get sick. Sometimes we get sick enough to die. I can think of several couples who had been married for many years and who deeply loved one another that demonstrated this. In each case, one of the partners got sick and died, but the other partner was in very good health. However, within just a few weeks or a few months, the other partner died also, seemingly for no good reason. But there was a reason – they grieved themselves to death, because they thought life was no longer worth living without their partner. Our physical health is tied to good grieving.

Most folks would recognize that grieving also affects us emotionally. After all, grief is all about feeling sad, hopeless, scared and alone. Throughout history there have been many different ways that people have tried to control grief, ignore grief and manage grief. None of these ways have seemed to help people work through grief, however.

There was an ancient philosophical group known as the Stoics who believed that the way to deal with any emotions, especially grief, was to simply ignore it and pretend that they did not feel anything.

This group is where we get the word, "stoical" from. They were the original stiff upper lip guys. They were the predecessors of the "macho false pride" groups of today. They might have even inspired the John Wayne theory of emotions – don't have any! This has never worked out and is not to be recommended as a way of dealing with grief.

Even members of the Christian Church have been sucked into this kind of stoical thinking on occasion. Christians have heard and come to believe that when they lose a loved one, they should not be sad, because after all, that person is "going to a better place", where they will have no suffering, no pain, no sickness, no sorrow and no more death. While I believe all that is true, it doesn't really do anything to help the family members and friends deal with the loss.

As Christians, we aren't worried about the loved one. We know that they are fine and as my father used to say, "They never had it so good". Grieving is always for us, for those left behind. We grieve for what we will no longer have and we wonder if we can go on without that person. There is a passage in the New Testament in 1 Thessalonians, chapter 4 that says, "Grieve not…" That's as far as many people get in hearing that passage and believe that if they grieve, they are showing a lack of faith. Actually, if they could listen a little further, the passage says, "Grieve not as those who have no hope". So, it doesn't mean that we shouldn't grieve. By all means, if we have something to grieve, do a good job of grieving. It just means that when we grieve, we should not do it like those who have no hope, because we have great hope in the resurrection of the dead and the life everlasting. But we will still hurt in the meantime.

Even if we know how to grieve in a healthy way and do that, it will take a considerable amount of time to work through a major loss. People who study these things, like Elizabeth Kubler-Ross and others have observed that it takes about two years to move through the various stages of grief to finally get to some acceptance and feel alright again. It is important to note that it takes two years if the person is dealing with their feelings of loss on a regular basis and in healthy ways. It does not mean that just because two years pass, the person will automatically be done grieving. If the loss is not shared over and over again, the grieving could go on indefinitely.

There is an old saying that many of us grew up with that goes like this: "time heals all wounds". It turns out that this is only half right, because time alone will not heal all wounds. It takes talking about our losses over time that will heal all wounds. So, one cannot simply talk a whole lot about their loss for one day or one week and then be over it. Nor can we simply let time go by without talking about the loss and expect to come to some acceptance. Both elements must be present for good grieving. We must talk about our loss again and again over a period of some time. The old saying would be much more accurate if it said, "time and talk heal all wounds".

During the years that I worked on the inpatient drug/alcohol unit in our hospital it became very evident that one way of looking at what we were doing is helping people to begin the grieving process over the loss of their first love, booze and drugs. There was great wisdom in how the program was set up, because we had a two year Aftercare Program, where patients and their family members would come to group therapy once per week and deal with the ongoing struggles of recovery. Remember that it takes two years to work through a major loss and that is what the addicts and codependents were doing, grieving their losses and coming to some acceptance.

There are some fairly predictable stages of grieving and those of us on the staff at the treatment center were able to readily detect these stages as patients moved through them. Grief expert Elizabeth Kubler-Ross listed these stages for dying patients and saw a progression of denial, anger, bargaining, depression and acceptance. My own observations for addicted patients moving through the stages of grief see the same basic struggles, with some variations.

The first stage that I have seen in this process I would call "Shock and Denial". Sometimes when facing a major loss, people will be in shock and then in denial, but sometimes it is the other way around, so I just lump them together. Shock is the mind's way of limiting the impact of the bad news that just hit you. There is a numbness that descends over the mind and body that can make grieving people look like zombies at this time. It seems that it is hard to focus and there is a sense of unreality about everything. I have seen this look when, as a chaplain, I have been called to the Emergency Department and am present with a person whose loved one has just been pronounced dead from an automobile accident. I have seen a similar look when I was the Nicotine Dependency Counselor in the hospital and a patient's Doctor came in to announce that the patient had lung cancer and must quit smoking immediately. There was shock, not only with the cancer diagnosis, but shock also from the news that the patient would have to quit smoking cigarettes.

Denial is another way to keep from feeling the full force of a blow that life has dealt you when you have a loss of something or someone that is very important to you. The first words people utter upon hearing about a devastating loss are words like, "no, it can't be" or "I can't believe it". Even when we know it could be and it is; we can't help ourselves from this kind of denial. We may even think we are prepared for a loss and expect it, but we almost always find out that there is no way to prepare for a loss, because it isn't a loss until it is gone. We don't want to accept loss, because we are not sure how we can go on without the person or thing we love. Denial helps us hold onto the illusion that nothing has to change in our life.

Funeral homes can be helpful in breaking through this denial of death when we have lost a loved one, because they begin the rituals of finality. These rituals include: making the arrangements for the burial plot, picking out the casket, planning the service, choosing music and choosing pallbearers. These activities help folks come to grips with the loss and break through some of the denial.

However, there is no time limit to this stage of grief or any of the other stages for that matter. I remember going to the home of a couple that had lost a son 7 years earlier in a drowning accident. They showed me their son's room and it was exactly the way it had been the day he had died. It was a room that they never used and was sort of a shrine to their son. They still could not talk about the loss after 7 years.

The next stage of grief I simply call "grieving". I recognize that the whole process is really grieving, but I like this word to describe what goes on here. "Grieving" describes the more active parts of grieving. It is when the reality hits that the person or thing that we love is gone and is not coming back. This is the stage where all the feelings that have been dammed up come gushing out.

This stage includes anger usually. Remember that we said that anger leaves us better defended than hurt or fear, so people usually go to anger after denial. I hear the anger over and over in the hospital and at funerals. Phrases like, "Why did she have to die" are commonplace. "How could God let this happen", is another standard response? "How could he leave me all alone like this" is frequently heard?

Oftentimes family members and friends will feel very guilty at a time of loss. We may think of the last words spoken and might remember them as harsh words and wish we had one more day to say the right things. Even if the relationship was good, we usually still feel somewhat guilty and think we maybe should have done more.

Another part of this active grieving stage is bargaining with God. We might think and say things like "If only you let her live, I'll be good and even go back to church". We might ask God to take us and let our loved one live. We might promise to never say another hateful thing again if only this loss isn't real.

When none of these things work, we usually fall into depression. There seems to be no hope. We despair and can find no purpose in anything we would normally do. People can make some very poor decisions at this point. I remember one man whose wife had died suddenly that said, "I think I'll just quit my job and move to Oregon. What difference does any of this make anymore without Susie?" This depression is not clinical depression and thus, is not mental illness. This is situational depression and can be relieved when the grieving is completed and the situation is different.

This "Grieving" stage of grief is a roller coaster of emotions from anger to guilt to bargaining to depression that washes over us and then after a while, washes over us again. It is a little like standing in the ocean with your back to the surf. A wave comes from behind and knocks you down on your face, grinding it into the sand. You get up spluttering and wonder where that wave came from, because you didn't see it coming. Then you are alright for a while and then another wave washes over you again and does the same thing. Eventually, in good grieving, the waves get less frequent and less powerful.

The next stage is "Trying to return to normal". We can only sustain powerful emotions for so long until we are all cried out and all wrung out. For example, we realize after the death of a loved one that we have to go back to work, mow the lawn, wash the dishes and pay the bills. So, that is what we do. We are still wondering what is the point of all this, but we just keep putting one foot in front of the other in a numb, mindless way and hope that something might matter again someday.

Eventually, if we do good grieving, we will come to some acceptance of our loss. This is much different than just admitting that we have had a loss. Admitting is done with teeth clenched together; accepting is done with teeth unclenched. Accepting is not just recognizing that we have had a loss, but being alright with that loss. We are at peace now and can talk about the loss and about the relationship without falling apart. Accepting means that we have been reminded that life is short and we need to get the most meaning out of it that we can. We can go on in life without our true love and life still has meaning.

If we are really good at grieving there can be another stage after acceptance and that is to actually see opportunity in loss. For example, I talked to a man who had been blinded in a farm accident by chemicals. He had worked through his grief and was then able to tell me that it was a really fortunate thing that he had become blind, because he could now see things that he never saw when he had physical sight. He spent more time and better time with his children now. He had very rewarding work with other people who had recently lost their sight.

I have met many people that went through the agony of divorce, but grieved the loss, made some changes in themselves and eventually found the soul mate that they were looking for. There was opportunity in that loss.

A friend of mine looked back on the loss of security as his job was phased out, but then said it was a real opportunity for him. He said that he would have never started his own business if he had not lost that job. He now loves what he is doing and is happier than ever.

All of these stages of grief are present in recovery from addiction and that is why I say that one way of looking at recovery is that it is one giant grief and loss process.

The shock and denial are always there in addiction and recovery. In fact, denial is the number one symptom of the disease. An addict is a person who has a disease whose number one symptom is that it keeps telling him that he does not have a disease – it's the rest of the world that's off! We talked about some of the various forms of denial earlier such as" minimizing, rationalizing and blaming. All of these will be employed by an addict to keep from experiencing the loss of their beloved addictive agent.

When pressed by others about having a problem, then the next stage of grieving comes into play with anger, bargaining and depression. I actually saw all of these things in one group therapy session recently. A middle-aged male patient started with "It really pisses me off that everybody thinks I have a problem with alcohol and drugs." After some confrontation he recognized why people might think that he had a problem and then he said, "Well, I'm willing to give up the alcohol, because that gets me in trouble with the law. But I shouldn't have to give up pot, because I don't get rowdy with pot – I just mellow out". After some more group confrontation about cross-dependency, the man concluded group by saying, "Oh, what's the use. I might as well just tell you all that I am going to quit everything and then be miserable and bored the rest of my life."

But the good news is that many addicted persons do come to some acceptance in the loss of their addictive agent. They recognize that what is gone is gone and it cannot come back without problems and are alright with that. They resign themselves to the fact that they are going to have to deal with pain and problems some other way than chemically. They are not grinding on it anymore and are glad that they are straight and sober.

If a person in recovery does some really good grief work, they can get to the stage of seeing opportunity in loss. They can understand that all the struggle that they went through to get clean and sober was well worth it, because the new life they have is not only far better than what they had, but is better than they could have ever had if they had not become an addict.

I remember a recovering friend of mine telling a group that he was very glad that he was an addict. One of the audience members asked him if that meant that he was glad that he was in recovery from addiction. He replied, "No, I'm glad that I am an addict, because without becoming addicted, I would have never needed recovery and without recovery I would never have found a spiritual way by which to live and this life is great! You can see that the grieving is completed.

There is great irony in addiction. People use chemicals in order to try to deal with loss in their life. But then the very thing that is supposed to take care of grief causes more grief. Then there is need for recovery and that recovery becomes another huge grieving process.

10
Codependency

The companion illness that goes along with dependency is codependency. If dependency is being addicted to a particular thing, then codependency would be someone who is addicted to an unhealthy person. Another way of saying that is that a dependent person is hooked on a substance and a codependent person is hooked on a person in an unhealthy way.

Codependency is a condition of low self-worth and shame. Very often codependents come from families of dysfunction and many of the things that we will talk about for adult children of dysfunction will also apply to codependents. There are several common characteristics of codependency. We will look at each of these separately to paint the picture of what codependency is and what it needs.

One issue that always surfaces in codependency is that a person will have difficulty with boundaries. Codependents have difficulty saying "no" to anyone, even when they want to say "no". I know of a couple that live here in central Indiana that are so bad at saying "no" that when their doorbell rings, they both literally duck behind the couch and wait for a period of time. Then one of them goes over and peeks around the curtain to see who is outside. If the person walking away is somebody that they would want to see, they open the door and say, "Oh, we're here"! However, if the person is someone they do not know, they just let them keep on walking.

The reason that they go through this elaborate charade, is because they are both so codependent and have such trouble establishing boundaries, that if the door opens and it is somebody selling something, they know that they will have to buy it, whether they want it or not, because they can't say "no". Their self worth is not high enough to believe that they could turn anybody down, so they just avoid people to avoid spending money they do not want to spend. This seems like a rather extreme example, but these are real people with a real problem. I happen to know that both of them grew up in households that had alcoholism, not coincidentally.

The lack of boundaries might show up in employment situations. A codependent person might let his or her employer take advantage of them. They might not be able to refuse special requests to work late, work on holidays and work in the place of others. They might not realize that they have a right to set limits and say that enough is enough. Very often codependency leads to becoming a workaholic. They may share a little too much with their co-workers and do some inappropriate self-disclosure if another worker shows any interest in them. They may come off as weak, fragile and a push-over. Or they may go to the other extreme and come across as distant, aloof or unfriendly.

Boundary issues in codependency usually seem to go to extremes without finding much middle ground. If you envision your own personal boundaries as being like a fence around your house, you can see what the problem of codependency is. The one extreme is that your fence is lying flat on the ground and has totally been destroyed. Oftentimes this is a result of our boundaries being violated when we were young. It is a very diffuse boundary at best. This fence cannot keep anybody or anything out. If you had cows like I do at home, those cows could walk right up onto your porch and drop a steaming pile of cow flopper right by your front door, because there is nothing there to stop them.

The other extreme would be that you would build a fence that is 15 feet high and 3 feet thick, with razor wire and cut glass on the top of it. This fence has no gate in it. This fence may look to you like a fortress, because nobody can get in to hurt you. However, it doesn't take long and you realize that it is not a fortress - it is a prison. Nobody may be able to get in to hurt you, but nobody can get in to help you either. But even worse than that is the fact that you can't get out!

Another of the core issues of codependency is self-esteem. If we have codependency, we will feel that we are not worthy of being in healthy relationships, or any relationships at all. We might have the sense that we are a fraud and somebody might find out some day who we really are. We tend to become "human doings" rather than "human beings", because we get our self-worth from what we accomplish, make, do and look like. We may become a perfectionist and try to do everything just so, in order that people won't notice that we, as a person, are not alright. Perfectionism covers shame and we try to do right in order to feel right, or at least be viewed by others as alright. Nothing is ever quite good enough as a result of this perfectionism. We might cover our own inadequacies by being judgmental and critical of others who don't do things as correctly as we do. We may try to curry favor in others by becoming people-pleasers. We may use giving as a way of staying safe in a relationship. The unhealthy thinking behind this is that if we give and give and give in a relationship, then that other person could never find anyone else who would be there for them that much, therefore, they can never dump us.

If we have codependency issues, another important aspect is caretaking of others. It is a good thing to care about others. It is a good thing at times to take care of others. But it is not a good thing to take care of others to the exclusion of ourselves. Caring about others shows that we have empathy and can get outside of our own issues and problems and be concerned about others. Also, there are times when we need to take care of others. When we have children, as parents we must take care of these offspring, because they are our responsibility, since we made them and because they cannot do this for themselves. On the other end of the age spectrum, there might be times when we have to take care of aging parents, because they cannot do for themselves. All of that is fine. But when we start taking care of others that can take care of themselves, we have slopped over into codependency.

Another aspect of caretaking of others is that we would not take care of ourselves. We might not even think we are worthy of having needs of our own. We have trouble asking for help for ourselves. We are more than willing to help other people, even without being asked, but we would feel somehow less as a person if we were to have to ask for help. Therefore, we oftentimes present ourselves as being just fine, even though everything is not fine.

We probably will not take the time to do even basic things for ourselves, like eat meals and go to the bathroom. I personally know of several nurses in our hospital that have had urinary tract infections mainly because they won't even take time to pee. It is a good thing to be busy going about the business of taking care of your patients if you are a nurse, but not to the exclusion of peeing! Self-care is important in the ability to take care of another as well. When we try to get all our emotional needs met by taking care of others, we are in trouble for codependency.

If we have codependency we will most likely be very loyal to our family, to our job, to our friends and especially to the addict in our life. We will be more loyal than loyalty deserves. We will be loyal even when there is no need to be loyal. The phrase "Through hell and high water" was probably invented for codependents.

Another part of codependency is having difficulty with balance in our lives. Like our addicted counterparts, if we have codependency, we will tend to live life in the extremes. Wide swings of emotion become the norm and extremes of behavior are common. We might go from super competent to very helpless. We might be very rigid in one instance, but very permissive in another. We fear failure, but sabotage our own success. We have trouble letting go and having fun. We can become addicted to excitement.

I have noticed something interesting about the nurses in our hospital. We have some outstanding nurses and they do a great job of taking care of our patients. However, after working in the hospital for 33 years, I have gotten to know many of the nurses personally. It is amazing to me how many of them are either in a relationship with an addict or come from a family of addiction and dysfunction. It is surely a disproportionate number who fall into these categories compared to the rest of the population. The percentages are skewed even higher if you are talking about nurses who either work in the Emergency Department or are Intensive Care Nurses.

It makes sense when you think about it though. Nurses are being paid to take care of people, so those caretaking skills and tendencies fit right into their job. Not only that, but there is an excitement in working in the Intensive Care and Emergency areas that meets the need for external stimulation and excitement. Every time I am called to the Emergency Department and watch those nurses hustle around amidst the pressure to give care immediately, because seconds count in near-death situations, I think that there must be something in their background that prepares them for this insanity. When I listen to the chaos of weeping family members and wailing spouses as these nurses efficiently go about the tasks of saving lives, I wonder how they were trained, not just in nurses training, but at home. My hunch is that the chaos of those areas of the hospital feels just like home. That is apparently their version of "normal".

My mother was an adult child of an alcoholic father and it strikes me as no coincidence that she entered nurses training and became a registered nurse after my sister and I were born. She worked as an industrial nurse for the Caterpiller Corporation for a number of years and used to tell stories of wondering what kind of trauma was going to come through the door from the manufacturing area. Was she going to be faced with a worker that just got his hand cut off? Was she going to deal with a heart attack? Or was it just going to be the usual piece of steel in a worker's eye? That kind of chaos would have driven anybody else nuts, but my mother was able to take it all in stride because of the training in dysfunction and chaos that she had at home.

Yet another area of codependent tendencies is in the area of perfectionism and control. We talked earlier about perfectionism being a cover-up for shame. People who live with addicts take on a great deal of shame for how their family members behave. There is a need to excuse and cover up bad behavior. Wives and husbands who are married to alcoholics or drug addicts feel strongly that their spouse is a reflection of who they are, so their clothing and personal appearance need to have close attention. Even though the codependent might have grown up with chaos, they still try to control situations to prevent chaos from being noticed by others.

The need to control in codependency is very strong. Let's take for example a wife who has an addicted husband. She knows that she can't control his drinking, drug usage, gambling, etc. so she sets about to control everything else around her. Her home will be scrubbed to within an inch of its life, her appearance will be flawless and she will be involved in several charitable enterprises to uphold the honor of the family. She will tend to try to influence people to do things her way and might be very upset if others don't want to do it that way. All of this need to control makes sense if you remember that the main frustration is feeling out of control because of the addiction in your family.

Sometimes codependents will become sympathy-seeking and allow others to see how difficult their life is because of addiction in the family. I remember a couple that I worked with years ago in North Dakota at the Human Service Center. I will call them Bill and Mary (not their real names). Bill had been drinking heavily for the 20 years of their marriage. Mary thought at the time that she married him that Bill would grow out of his drinking phase after he was a married man and was settled down, but that did not happen. He never settled down. His drinking got worse and caused her great embarrassment. They lived in a small town that was founded and populated with mostly German/Russian immigrants. These people knew all about Bill's wild escapades when drinking and began to feel very sorry for Mary. If you went to the local cafe, and Bill and Mary came in, you could always hear folks say after they left, "Oh, that Mary. Such a saint she is to put up with that Bill and his damnable drinking"!

But one day Bill ended up going into inpatient drug/alcohol treatment. It was not due to Mary's complaining or long-suffering looks, however. Bill wound up in treatment because his employer had enough of his hung-over performances and absenteeism. Bill's boss gave him what I call "the Godfather offer". It goes like this, "Bill, do you like having a job here? Well, then you're going to love treatment"!

Bill did alright in treatment, but he really found it in the fellowship of Alcoholics Anonymous. He got a good sponsor, attended meetings, did his daily readings faithfully and worked on his spiritual growth as he worked the 12 Steps. In just two years he was a very different man than he had been and was a good husband, involved father and responsible worker. However, guess what Mary did after those two years of his sobriety? That's right, she divorced Bill!

You see, Mary had lost her sainthood. People were no longer saying, "Oh, that Mary, such a saint she is…" She wasn't putting up with anything anymore. She had a good husband and was faced with possibly dealing with an adult relationship with a healthy man. She couldn't take it.

The end of the story is that it only took her a year to find another man and marry him and you are probably not wondering just what kind of man this might be. That's right, she found another alcoholic! Then the folks at the cafe were saying, "Oh, poor Mary, she is so unlucky to have gotten out of a relationship with one drinker, just to get into a relationship with another drinker". But Mary wasn't just unlucky - she was sick. She needed somebody sick to take care of and control and she wanted her sainthood back, because she couldn't see that others could value her just for herself, even if she didn't have "bad luck".

There is that sick part of the addict in a codependent's life that really likes to see the progression of sickness in codependents, because that protects their own using. So, if you are a drug addict and your wife is getting sainthood out of your disease, that works out very nicely, because she certainly needs a sinner to take care of to maintain that sainthood.

When an addict senses the uncertainty and low self-worth in his or her codependent partner, they know they are now free to do anything they want and nothing will be done about it. The more uncertain and crazy the codependent, the more license the addict has to keep on keeping on.

There is even a technique that I have seen used many times by addicts with spouses that I call "addicted crazy-making". This usually involves a series of statements and actions that undermine the spouse's confidence. One of the more extreme examples of this was another couple that I worked with years ago. The husband was an alcoholic and his wife had tried to talk to him about quitting drinking or at least cutting down (as if he could). He was getting very tired of her pleas and complaints about his drinking, so he set about ruining her self-image and confidence.

She happened to be one of those people that was a very sound sleeper and was so groggy when she woke up that she didn't know if she was afoot or on horseback for at least a half

hour after awakening. Her husband would get up, go downstairs and prepare some breakfast cereal for himself. Then he would hide the milk in one of the cupboards. When the wife came dragging down to eat breakfast, she poured her corn flakes and then opened the refrigerator to get the milk out, but there was none in there. "Oh no", she said, "We don't have any milk for the cereal". "Yes we do", the husband retorted. "Well, I don't see any in there", she replied. "It's in the cupboard where you put it", he responded. She looked in the cupboard, dazed and confused and there was the milk.

The conclusion of this story is that the next time the wife started to say something about how crazy her husband's drinking was, he shot back verbally at her saying, "So, you think I'm crazy for doing a little drinking, huh? Well at least I'm not so crazy that I don't know where I put the milk in the morning"! Her confidence was so eroded by the time I met this couple that she wasn't sure of anything anymore. The only reason they had to come to see me is because the husband had his third DUI and had to have a drug/alcohol assessment. He certainly wasn't there because his wife had any influence on him. She had lost the ability to confront any bad behavior long ago because of the alcoholic crazy-making.

Basically, codependency means that one is living a second-hand life. If I am the codependent person in an addicted or dysfunctional relationship, I don't think about my own needs, my own opinions or my own problems. I think about the addict's feelings, needs and issues.

I remember talking to a married couple where the husband was a drug addict and the wife was very codependent. Whenever I asked the wife a question, she looked at her husband to answer it. I finally had to ask her to answer her own questions, but she still couldn't do it without first looking at her husband for approval to do so. She looked like a woman that had been beaten down verbally and physically enough that she knew when to keep her mouth shut. She was not going to confront her husband and would instead take the blame for his actions.

This wife was so sick that when one of the children told about a time that dad had come home from work and been in a rage and had thrown the food and the dishes all over the kitchen, she took the blame. She said, "I know that he likes to have the food all ready at 5:00 when he gets home from work and I didn't do it and was late, so that was my fault. She also admitted that she had bought a new winter coat, because her other one was falling apart, but thought another rage episode was caused by her doing that and spending money on herself. She added that maybe if she had sex with him every day instead of just five times per week, that he would be happy and wouldn't get so mad.

Codependents often feel responsible for the problem user that they are involved with and feel guilty for not being able to do something to fix things. Many times attempts to control the usage will lead to things like: taking over financial control in the family, denying affection to manipulate the addict into change, asking the addict to promise that they will be good and making threats that are never backed up by any behavior.

There are usually signs of mental strain as part of codependency. Most of a codependent's thoughts revolve around the addicted person and the problems they are causing. There is an obsession to find something that will make the addicted person change. There can be loss of sleep over trying to deal mentally with this problem in the relationship. There can be withdrawal from outside activities and friends because of the shame over the chemical abuse by the addict in the family.

Physical symptoms can start to appear from the toll that the addictive disease is taking for those around the addict. Dizziness, nausea, stomach ulcers, diarrhea or constipation, shakiness, sweating and chewed off fingernails are very common in those affected by the illness of addiction.

In fact, many times those people who are in a codependent position get sicker than the addict himself or herself. The reason this happens is because the addict is anesthetized with drugs, alcohol or their brains own feel good chemicals. Those around the addict in the family are not anesthetized, however and feel all the pain. It would be a little like two people going into the hospital for heart surgery, one of whom is given anesthesia before the operation and the other of whom is not. Which one of these patients is going to feel more pain and be affected more? Obviously, it is the one that has no anesthesia. This is the position that codependents are in with an addict in their life. They feel all the pain, the shame, the anger and the fear while the addict goes on her merry way, blissfully unaware of the wreckage left behind.

There is a funny, but tragic picture of this situation given in the Big Book of Alcoholics Anonymous. The section says that the alcoholic is like a tornado sweeping through people's lives, leaving buildings flattened and lives destroyed. Then the alcoholic comes up out of the storm cellar and doesn't see the wreckage or even wonder how it got that way. He just says, "Ain't it grand that the wind stopped blowing, Ma"?

The addict is most often genuinely surprised to find out that her addiction was really affecting others that much. They have really believed that they have not been hurting anybody else and can't fathom why others are so upset over their addictive ways. I had an alcoholic woman say in group one day, "Well, I don't know why my family is bitching all the time about my drinking. The only person I'm hurting is myself". She actually believed that until she had some clean time and saw the tread marks on her family member's faces where she had run over them, backed up and hit it again.

So, under the umbrella of the addictive illness we see both the afflicted and the affected. There are those folks who are afflicted with the disease of addiction and those around the addict who are affected by the disease. That includes the codependents who are living with an addicted person and the Adult Children of Addicts who grew up with addiction and are still affected by it even after growing up and leaving home.

Thus, there are those sick persons who are going down the toilet of life because of their disease and then there are those who are swirling down the toilet with them and becoming just as sick. That is why codependents need their own separate recovery.

11

Adult Children of Dysfunction

The third group of people who would fall beneath the umbrella of the disease of addiction would be people who grew up in a family where there was addiction and are now struggling, as adults, with the damage done to them as they were growing up. This group is often called ACOA's, which stands for Adult Children of Addicts. A term that would be a little more inclusive would be ACOD, which stands for Adult Children of Dysfunction. This term includes not only people who have been raised in drug and alcohol affected families, but also children who grew up with parents addicted to rage, work and sexual deviancies.

Not all people raised in dysfunction are alike, but they tend to have many characteristics in common. One of the foundational feelings caused by growing up in dysfunction is shame. As you recall from the chapter on shame, if we have shame it means that we feel that we are not o.k., not good or good enough, that we are bad, wrong and should not exist. Children who grow up in some kind of dysfunction have the feeling that something is not right in their family, but they don't have much to compare it to, so they assume that it must be themselves who are wrong. After all, big people are telling them that whatever is going on in the family is their fault and since they are big people, they must be right, which means that the child must be wrong!

An example I used in group therapy one day illustrates this. I told the patients that I came from the bluff country of Southeastern Minnesota. It has become a tourist area and people rent bicycles and rollerblades to go on the state trail that ran through our farm and rent canoes and inner tubes to float down the river. I said, "Imagine if when I was a small child, every day my father went out into the woods and waited behind a tree alongside the trail until a cyclist came along and then he jumped out and whacked them over the head. Then he dragged them home, boiled them up in a big pot and we ate them for supper. Now, what do you think would seem normal to me as a kid?" One of the patients said, "I guess cannibalism would seem normal to you, but that's just sick"!

He was right; that is just sick, but the point here is that my version of "normal" is whatever I grew up with or got used to and your version of "normal" is whatever you grew up with or got used to. My "normal" is not necessarily going to be the same as everyone else's "normal". But more importantly, if I grew up in a home that was well beyond the bounds of what most folks would consider "normal", that is going to affect me in a lot of ways when I become an adult.

I remember an incident when I was about 8 and my sister was 11. We went to visit our cousins for an afternoon at their house. These cousins were each about a year older than we were. We played with them for a while and were having a good time, but then their parents came home and started fighting with each other. They were saying words to each other that my sister and I had never heard at our house. They were saying words we never heard in Sunday School either. The volume of their yelling and the cussing and mentioning of certain body parts was a whole new, shocking thing to us. We looked at our cousins and wondered what in the world could be going on, but they just looked at us and said, "Don't worry about it, mom and dad are just fighting again". It didn't even seem to faze them anymore, so we figured that this probably wasn't the first time they had ever experienced something like this. We, on the other hand, were traumatized. We went back home and replayed and talked about this scary and bizarre visit for days. We were reluctant to even tell our parents about it, for fear that they would think we were making stuff up or overreacting.

As we said in the chapter on shame, when adults act shamelessly, it shames children, because they feel something is wrong and their egocentric brain tells them it must be them that is in the wrong. They don't know that there are other families who operate in a different way from their sick family, just like my sister and I didn't know that there were families that acted differently from our healthier family.

Adult Children of Dysfunction have learned to somehow adjust to the weirdness in their families. Whenever I see the advertising for the television program, "Survivor", I always think that the show should be made up entirely of Adult Children of Dysfunction, because they are above all else, survivors. They have survived physical abuse, verbal abuse, sexual abuse and spiritual abuse. They have survived the flip side of the coin of abuse, which is neglect. They have been ignored, locked in closets, given no recognition and given no helpful instruction in life. They have been given very little of what a child needs to grow up healthy and yet have somehow managed to still exist. They did not have loving boundaries, healthy touch, encouragement, safety and fun. They had fear, shame, criticism and neglect.

The problem is that some of the survival skills that they learned don't translate well to the rest of the world that is not as dysfunctional. I have a story about survival skills that seems to help patients understand what their dysfunctional training has done to them.

The story is that there was a young man who was on a tall wooden sailing vessel many years ago. The ship ran into a terrible storm and went down, killing all aboard, except the young man. He managed to float to shore on a piece of the broken ship. He found that he was on a deserted island. There was plenty of fruit to eat and some roots, but there were not many animals for meat. However, there seemed to be lots of cats on the island. The young man assumed that the cats were left off by other ships that had stopped there in the past, because ships always carried cats to keep the mouse and rat population in check down in the hold where the grain was stored. These cats were everywhere on the island and some of them were fairly tame. The young man began thinking about them as a source of meat and began harvesting them on a regular basis to supplement his diet.

Many years later another ship came by and saw his signal fire and picked the young man up and took him back to England and home. There was a great celebration by his relatives, friends and neighbors and they found him a fascinating person, because of all his island experiences. There was only one thing that was disturbing in his neighborhood and that was that several neighbors noticed that their cats were missing! To their horror, they eventually found out what was happening to them. The young man was eating them just like he had done on the island.

This story is similar to what happens to people who grow up in addiction and dysfunction. They learn certain survival skills growing up in the craziness, but these survival skills just don't work in other healthier places.

The same thing happens to men and women who are in prison for prolonged periods of time. They learn certain survival skills in prison that usually include: showing no fear, becoming hardened to others, violence and self-centeredness. They are forced to do these things or else get victimized by beatings and prison rape. However, when they get out of prison and are trying to adjust to life outside the walls, these same survival skills don't translate very well in dealing with people who don't have their same experiences.

An example of this different way of thinking comes from a 35 year old man who was in treatment for his alcohol and marijuana addiction. He was lamenting the fact that even though he had a good job and made lots of money, he never seemed to have enough to pay his bills. He said that he could easily cover the money he spent on booze and pot, because he did some dealing of the pot and basically got that for free. But he never had any cash on hand for when emergencies came up like a hospital bill or a car repair bill or something like that. He blew his money as fast as it came in.

I was sitting there listening to this and wondering why he didn't just take the cash out of his savings account to cover these emergencies. That's what my family trained me to do. Whenever we got extra money as kids from birthdays, Christmas or from selling our cattle, my father would always insist that we put it into our savings accounts right away, because he said that you never knew when you might need this for "a rainy day".

But this young man had not grown up in my family and that was not his version of "normal". Every day was a rainy day in his family. He said that his father was an alcoholic and he and his siblings learned very quickly that if they had two nickels to rub together, they had better immediately take them down to the store and buy some candy or a toy with it, because if Dad came home and was thirsty, he would scour the house and take whatever money there was and go get drunk on it. This also included the children's money.

What this young man described was learned impulsiveness. He and his brothers and sisters found out that you might as well "eat, drink and be merry, for tomorrow we may die" or maybe it would be more correct to say, "Eat, drink and be merry, for soon Dad will come home and take everything we have". There was no sense of looking ahead and coming up with a plan of action that might lead to a greater gain later on. There was only a resolve to do what we can do now, because it will be taken away and we'll get nothing.

Another woman in this same group, who was also an ACOA, said that she knew just how that young man felt. She shared that in her family her father was also an alcoholic and she and her sister never knew what the rules in the home were going to be from day to day. She said that if her father was drunk, there was one set of rules, albeit not well defined, but if he was sober there was a different set of rules. And if he was trying to be sober for a little while and hadn't been drinking for some time, there was yet another set of rules. They never knew which rules they were going to have, so if there was a chance to do something one day, you had better get right on that and do it, because the next day it was denied.

She went on to describe how these rules worked. She said that if Dad was fairly intoxicated, he seemed to relax all the rules. If she wanted to go and stay overnight with her friend or go downtown and hang out with the kids or go to a ballgame, she would try to catch him when he was pleasantly woozy, but not yet at the point of being "mean drunk". She said that at these times if she had asked to take the car and drive to Las Vegas with her boyfriend at age 15, he would have said, "Yeah, go ahead; I don't care". When he was not drinking, he had what would be considered more regular and sane household rules. But the worst time to ask for something or try to do something she wanted was when her father had not been drinking for some time and was on a "dry drunk" and was "meaner than a snake". At these times it didn't matter what she wanted to do; the answer was going to not just be "no", but "hell no"!

For people who grew up in dysfunction there is very little inclination to delay immediate gratification for a greater gain later on. In the first place, if you wait and try to save, it will just get taken away from you, as we said. But in the second place, there just isn't much belief that there could be any greater gain later on. There is just one disappointing thing after another. As one of our patients in treatment summed it up, "Don't worry, nothing's going to turn out alright"! Another addict who grew up in an addicted family gave us the true sense of hopelessness that accompanies addicted families by saying, "Yeah, that's right, life is just a crap pie and every day I eat another slice"!

Part of this hopelessness and lack of expectation of anything positive also comes from the culture of poverty. The culture of addiction and the culture of poverty oftentimes go hand in hand. They aren't always one and the same, but they are closely related, because generations of addiction are what got that family into the culture of poverty sometimes. I spent five years as the Nicotine Dependency Counselor at our hospital and it was always interesting to me to listen to the reasons why people could not quit using tobacco. Physicians would order me to do a consultation on tobacco users and assess what their needs might be and try to motivate them to use the resources available and quit tobacco. I recall one middle-aged man who had Chronic Obstructive Pulmonary Disease and came from a family of addicts. His Dr. had told him that if he did not quit smoking cigarettes, that there was really nothing that could be done for him and he was doomed to a horrible, gasping, lingering death.

I felt he should be sufficiently motivated for recovery by this speech by his physician and was ready to help him in any way I could. After the assessment I asked if he was ready to quit tobacco and he said that he would like to, but the physical withdrawal just drove him crazy and he always relapsed very quickly when he had tried before. I suggested that he use a nicotine replacement product like nicotine patches, nicotine gum or nicotine inhaler to stave off the physical symptoms of withdrawal. He said that might work, but he couldn't really afford it. He said, "You know those nicotine patches cost about seventy dollars for a month's supply." "Well," I said, "You are smoking about two packs a day and that costs you almost two hundred dollars per month". "Yeah", he replied, "but you can buy those cigarettes one pack at a time and you have got to lay out the whole seventy dollars for those patches"!

At this point in my career I didn't even blink when I heard him say this, because I was used to this kind of thing. What used to make me think, "How short-sighted can you get", now just made me shake my head! I have seen it too many times to even be surprised anymore. The unwillingness to delay immediate gratification, the hopelessness, and the lack of loftier goals for life are all too familiar and are just part of the disease. I expect these symptoms just like I expect someone with a cold to have a snotty nose, stuffy head and fever.

Besides these survival skills there are many other negative factors in growing up with dysfunction. If you grew up in this situation, you might very well become phony, because you had to just guess at what "normal" should be and then you had to pretend to be that. There isn't a very clear sense of the core of your being in this guessing process. Many times ACOA's are guessing at "normal", but they are guessing wrong!

You will almost certainly have trouble in your relationships with ACOA background. Fear of your own unworthiness will surface and you will be insecure, even if your partner or friend is very trustworthy. You will begin to wonder when the rug is going to be pulled out from under you, since it always was when you were growing up in your relationships in your family of origin. As one patient in treatment expressed it, "I just keep wondering when my new boyfriend is going to dump me. He seems nice, but it always happens to me, so I don't want to put too much weight on this relationship right now." In these instances jealousy is common, because there is just not enough self-worth to believe that another would not want to jeopardize the relationship in any way.

Sometimes the jealousy and possessiveness becomes very extreme and ACOA's have been known to not so much have relationships, but to instead take hostages! There is a strong need to control one's relationships, which makes sense in a sick sort of way if you remember that being out of control is one of the major fears growing up in an addicted family. Oftentimes there is more loyalty than loyalty deserves in these relationships. ACOA's will hang in there in sick relationships in their families long after anything good ceased to come out of them.

Another attempt to stay safe in relationships is by people-pleasing. If you grew up in a dysfunctional family, one thing you feared and did anything to avoid was conflict. If you can avoid a scene by going along with whatever anyone else wanted, it seems a small price to pay at that time, but leads to a big price later on when you can't say "no" to anything. People-pleasing stems from the fear that if you are not liked, you will be abandoned and the way to be liked is to go along with the other person and do extra things to ingratiate yourself to the other.

Closely related to people-pleasing is perfectionism. As we said in the chapter on shame, perfectionism is a cover-up for shame. If I feel that I am not good enough, then I will have to do more good things. Maybe people will see all my good works and not notice that I am really a worthless piece of dung. We fear that people will find us out, so we scramble to do more and more things correctly to bolster our badly sagging self-image. We develop a strong need to be right - extremely right.

We might even try to physically look right at all times. Vanity is often another offshoot of perfectionism. If we look good, maybe folks won't notice that we really aren't good. An example of this is again my mother. She had an alcoholic father and the shame that goes with that spurred her on to try and look good at all times. She learned to sew at a very early age so that she would not look "dutchy" to her schoolmates, which meant out of fashion. When my sister and brother and I grew up, mom was always very careful to make sure that we had clothes that were in style. She checked the catalogues and magazines and kept up on the latest styles. Nobody could shame us for not being up with the times in the world of fashion, she reasoned. The problem with this was that we may have been in fashion in New York City or Chicago, but we lived on a farm in the middle of nowhere and jeans and work boots were in style where we came from. Consequently, we were the only ones in style, which didn't make us feel any more accepted or appreciated.

ACOA's also tend to be procrastinators. If you grew up in a household of dysfunction of some kind, you were probably never taught how to plan a project, get the necessary supplies and see the project through to its completion. I used to be able to pick out houses that had an ACOA alcoholic man living inside them. I would see the ditch dug in the back of the house where footings had been poured several years ago, but the room addition was never finished. There is a house in my area that has had bundles of shingles perched on top of the roof for over three years now, but the roof has never been shingled. Down that same road is a garden plot that was plowed up this spring, but nothing was ever planted. I can recall numerous business ideas that were started, but there was no follow-through and nothing ever came of them. I have subsequently learned that most of these situations do indeed have untreated Adult Children of Addicts residing there and most of them are also addicted themselves.

The opposite of this procrastinating is becoming a workaholic. People who fall under the umbrella of the addictive illness live life in the extremes, so one would expect to see behavior at both ends of the spectrum with very little middle ground and that is what does show up. A workaholic has a strong need to do and accomplish, which is an attempt to cover up shame again. ACOA's will sometimes work longer and harder than anyone else to look good, hard-working and competent so that others will not notice that they are really not good enough. The subconscious belief is that if they do good things, people might think that they are good.

My mother was a great ACOA example of this obsession with doing a lot and doing it right. There was nothing that she could not do and do in a hurry. She was quick-moving, decisive, competent and efficient. We used to tease her because her favorite phrase was "go and do". She would say, "Well, we could go and do this or maybe go and do that". If you wanted something done, all you had to do was enlist Lois Rissman and your worries were over, because the job was going to get done and it was going to be done right.

The downside of this attitude that my mother had is that it was difficult for her to let go and relax. She was not so much a "human being" as a "human doing" sometimes. I recall that I was at home in Minnesota for a visit and mom had gone through surgery and chemotherapy for breast cancer. She was recovering and seemed to be getting better, but I wanted to find out what dad thought about how she was doing physically. We went out to the barn, which is where most of the meaningful conversations take place. I asked dad, "How is mom doing anyway"? He was serious, for once and said, "Oh, the old mother isn't doing too well. She can only do the work of about one woman now!" He was not kidding and this was his honest assessment of how she was doing. By this comment I knew that mom had been reduced to about one-third of her usual physical strength and stamina, because she normally could get the work done of about three women.

Another poignant memory about mom is when her cancer came back several years later as bone cancer. She was reduced to only being able to walk a few steps and could do very little. Mostly, she just sat on the couch and watched television or talked on the phone, encouraging other people who were, as she said, "having a tough time". My sister and I took a trip to Minnesota to spend some time with her, because we knew that she was dying and it was a race to see if the cancer was going to kill her first or the congestive heart failure.

The day after we arrived, mom was sitting on the couch with a needle and thread and some clothing that needed to be altered next to her. She said, "Well, I think I could watch my program that I like on T.V. if I would work on this sewing while I watch". My sister said, "You know what mom - I think you could watch your program on T.V. even if you didn't work on any sewing". This apparently sounded like blasphemy to mom because she said rather vehemently, "Well, you can't just sit there and do nothing"! I suggested that you actually could do that, but mom never bought it until the day that she died. I really think that instead of having "Loving wife and mother" on her tombstone, we should have chiseled on there, "Well, you can't just sit there and do nothing". It would have been much more characteristic of who she was all her life.

Adult Children of Addicts have many of the same issues that we talked about in the chapter on codependency, because it really is a type of codependency. The attraction to chaos is very much a part of the negative aspects of ACOA's as well. As mentioned before, emergency room nurses, Doctors and techs have a very high incidence of either being in a codependent relationship or of having grown up in dysfunction. The drama feels just like home. One positive aspect of this however, is that these emergency room workers are very good at what they do and can handle the chaos better than the average worker and can be efficient, precise and not overwhelmed by the tragedy and stress of an emergency department.

Another negative result from growing up in dysfunction is a tendency toward self-pity. There is a sense that life isn't fair (which it isn't) and why does this stuff have to happen to me? Sometimes instead of finding solutions to problems that arise, ACOA's will just sit and spin their wheels and do nothing because the universe is picking on them. At times this self-pity also leads to difficulty having fun in life, because to have fun would seem like an admission that one doesn't need to stay in pity, because there can be some good things in life.

A kind of shorthand way at looking at what it is like to grow up in dysfunction is the way we used to describe the family rules of a dysfunctional family. The unwritten rules are: 1) Don't talk, 2) Don't trust and 3) Don't feel.

The first unwritten rule is usually pounded into the children's brains from the time they are little. One patient shared in group that the phrase he remembers most from growing up with his alcoholic father and codependent mother was "Now, this is our family business and nobody needs to know anything about our family business, so just keep your mouth shut, boy". Another patient chimed in by saying that the phrase in his family was "You don't need to go blabbing all over town what we do in this family. It's none of their business."

The second unwritten rule that is learned is not to really trust anybody, because they will ultimately let you down. You may have to use people from time to time to get what you want, but never put your complete trust in them, because you'll just get hurt again.

The third unwritten rule is to avoid all feelings whenever you can, because many feelings can leave you vulnerable and people can get inside you and hurt you worse. Just talk about your thoughts, but not your feelings.

There are so many negative consequences from growing up in a family of dysfunction, but there can be some positives that can come out of this unique experience as well. There seems to be two different ways that a child can go in growing up with dysfunction. One fork in the road is to view yourself as helpless, as a victim and as unable to make anything out of your life, because of the rough start you have had. The other fork in the road is to recognize that if anything good is going to happen, you are going to have to make it happen, because your family probably isn't going to help you do it and in fact will usually hinder you.

I refer back to my mother again as a perfect example of somebody who took the second fork in the ACOA road. She grew up in a pretty weird household. Her father, Leonard Thorp was Native American and Welsh and this genetic background made him a sitting duck for alcoholism. He was a very bright and talented man. He was very good with horses and folks used to bring their horses to Leonard instead of to a veterinarian when they had trouble with them. He was considered a kind of "horse whisperer" at the time. But despite these talents, he was a chronic alcoholic.

Leonard lost his first wife to illness and had lost his son in the First World War. My grandmother, Selma, was his housekeeper after his first wife died. Selma's parents came over from the old country (Norway) and didn't have a very enlightened notion of what women could do in life, so they offered her very little education. I believe she made it through the fourth grade. She could read and write, but that is about it. Her parents figured that she knew how to cook, clean and sew, so what else does a girl need? That is what she was doing for Leonard; cooking, cleaning and sewing.

Being the shrewd alcoholic that he was, Leonard eventually figured out that if he married Selma, she could do all the things she was doing for him then for nothing. Selma was very shy and backward and she probably saw it as her one chance to get married, so she took it. Leonard was 30 years older than she was when they married.

Even by the time that I was born, grandma Selma was still very intimidated by anything new or complex. For example, if you ever were given a phone message that grandma Selma wrote down, you might as well throw it away and wait for them to call back, because grandma would get so flustered at having to take the message that she had it all screwed up. She inherited the farm, but she never wrote a single check in her life for that business. My parents took care of everything financial and my father took care of dealing with the people who rented her farm. She never learned to drive and was very dependent on my parents. Grandma almost burned our house down by putting metal pots and pans in the new microwave oven. Anything new intimidated her.

This is the family that my mother was born into. Her father was 67 years old and her mother was 37 years old when she was born and they were 70 and 40 respectively when mom's brother, Bob was born. Her father was old and drunk and her mother was uneducated and backward.

Fortunately, mom took the fork in the ACOA road that led to a very productive life and not the road of self-pity. Mom figured out very early that if she was ever going to get to do anything that was worthwhile or fun, she was going to have to make it happen. Her motto was "If it is to be, it's up to me". She knew that her aging, drunk father was only interested in his own peace and quiet and was not going to go out of his way to assist her with anything that she wanted to do. She knew that her uneducated, shy mother would be too intimidated to try anything new with her either.

Mom knew that it had to be her own initiative that would lead her to a meaningful life and she went at it like she meant it. She accomplished so many things that I still wonder at her. My wife believes that I think my mother was perfect, which is not true. I know that she had many character defects from her dysfunctional background, even though she did work on these. No, I never thought that my mother was perfect, but I do believe that she was remarkable, especially considering the start that she had.

In High School she was a good student and a cheerleader. She learned how to play the piano and made a little money playing for a local church on Sundays. As I said before, she became an excellent seamstress and made all her own clothes.

She quit college to get married and had two children and then decided to go to nurses training to be a registered nurse. This was a groundbreaking move on her part, because at that time nobody was allowed into nurses training who was married, let alone married with children. She was the test case to see if women could really handle nurses training while having a family. This seems very odd to us today and when I tell nurses at our hospital about this they look at me in disbelief. But that's the way things were back in the 1950's. Mom, of course, did very well and graduated as one of the top nurses that they had at that time. Part of her ACOA background that was helpful was her determination to be successful at whatever she tried and to work to make that happen no matter what it took.

As her career went on mom was a health nurse at a University, an industrial nurse for the Caterpillar Corporation, a home health nurse, floor nurse and a psychiatric nurse. At the end of her career she even taught High School in the Health Occupations section of the Vocational School. In between these nursing jobs she did many other jobs. She was a bookkeeper for the John Deere Implement. She was a waitress at the local supper club. She was a regional manager for a life insurance company. She also had her own business selling cleaning products for some time.

In short, there was nothing that mom could not do; there were just things that she hadn't gotten around to yet. Twelve weeks before she died mom started taking art lessons, because it was something she had always wanted to try and of course, she was pretty good! Growing up in dysfunction spurred her on to make things happen in her life and she did.

Another positive from mom's ACOA background was the fact that she was always the champion of the underdog. If there was somebody at a function that seemed to be off by themselves and not interacting, mom was always the first one to go over, start talking to them and start introducing them to other people so they would be comfortable. If there was a student struggling in her class, mom was always spending extra time with her and encouraging her that she could do it. Her relationships with kids that came from problem homes were remarkable. At her funeral there were at least a dozen young people that came up to us and told stories of how they would have never believed that they could be nurses or Doctors or medical technicians if it were not for the encouragement they got from Lois Rissman.

When I made trips home I would always get talked into being a guest speaker for mom's health occupation classes, because I could fill the slots she had for clergy, chaplain and addiction counselor. But what amazed me was that mom could get these kids to do the amount of work that they did in her class. I had college courses that were not near as tough as this High School class. Somehow my mother was able to get these kids to see themselves through her eyes and see the great things that they could do. I do not think that any of this would have been possible without the struggles that mom went through in her own dysfunctional growing up days. She was always sensitive to other people's needs by remembering her own needs when she was their age.

People who grew up in similar situations to my mother oftentimes have the ability and the inclination to take care not only of themselves, but of siblings, aging parents and others in need. They often help their family of origin out not only emotionally, but financially.

So, there are some very positive things that can come out of the adversity of growing up in dysfunction. Actually, most people who do great things in life have had to fight through some major obstacles, so this is not surprising. However, as we said, there are some very negative aspects of coming out of dysfunction and the people who do positive things deserve a great deal of admiration, because they could have easily given up, wallowed in self-pity and said, "What can I do? I had a bad childhood!"

12
Family Roles

A phrase that I have heard many times by patients in drug/alcohol treatment is the following: "I don't know why my family is so upset; the only person I'm hurting is myself". Unfortunately, addicted persons actually believe this, even though it is patently untrue. On an average, an addict grossly affects at least four other persons and has a negative influence on several others. The self-centeredness that is part of this disease prevents addicts from seeing things from anybody else's perspective but their own. So, they go merrily on their way, running over those nearest them and have no notion of how those tread marks got on their faces.

There is usually an entire enabling system that surrounds the addicted person and everyone has a role that they play to keep the game going. If there are enough people in the family, it is easy to spot these various roles being played out. If there are less members of the family, sometimes spouses and children will take more than one role or if it is a large family, they may double up on some of the roles.

Let's use as our example an average addicted family with the father being addicted to alcohol, the mother being the codependent and chief enabler and four children, all of whom have a role in the family drama.

We already have discussed in previous chapters what the alcoholic will be doing – he will be drinking and working as hard as he can to not have anyone notice that this is a problem. He may be a perfectionist in order to cover his feelings of shame. He may work harder and longer than anyone else to show his family that he is really a responsible, hard-working dad who deserves a little relaxation from time to time that he gets out of a bottle. He may look good, talk good and smell good to stave off the dreaded day when people find out that he is not good and must change.

He may feel guilty and try to push blame off onto other people in the family so that his own behavior is forgotten. He may try to make up for the time he does not spend with his family by giving them material gifts. It is important for the addict to erode his family's self-confidence, so that they don't believe that they have the right to say anything about the addicts using behaviors. Whenever they try to bring up some of the negative effects of his drinking, the addict will immediately bring out a list of things that the others in the family are doing wrong. Eventually, the family members are trained to never say anything about the using, because it gets very unpleasant around the house when they do.

I refer back to my mother's dysfunctional family for an excellent example of yet another way of dealing with guilt. When I was growing up we had a very happy family, largely because my mother was smart enough to realize what she didn't know about parenting and listened to my father about how children should be raised. Fortunately, my father had great, loving, consistent parents and he knew what he was doing.

However, there were two days of the year that my siblings and I could always count on as being miserable days in our family and those days were Christmas and my mother's birthday. It seemed like no matter what my father tried to do for her or what kind of gift he got her, it was never right or never enough. My father grew up in the height of the Great Depression and his idea of a big Christmas as he was growing up was to get a pair of homemade socks and his sack of nuts and fruit at church on Christmas Eve. But he went overboard for mom, by his standards, getting much more than was reasonable, so that mom would be placated on Christmas and her birthday.

None of this silliness made sense to me as I was growing up until later on when I learned more about family systems and particularly addicted family systems. As I paid more attention to my mother's stories, it became clear to me what had happened to her. As you will recall, her father was old and drunk when mom was a child and her father had very little to do with the kids. In fact, when they would be running around, making some noise and being normal rambunctious kids, he would whack them with his cane as they went by.

However, even though the kids got very little of their father's attention during normal days, there were two days of the year when he went all out and bought them big gifts and lots of gifts and those days were, you guessed it, Christmas and their birthdays. These two days of the year were when their dad trotted out what I call the "alcoholic guilt gifts". These two days were to make up for the other 363 days of the year of unhealthy neglect.

Once I knew these stories and realized the significance of what was happening in the family system, it all made sense to me as to why we had such miserable days two times per year. My father never really had a chance to please mom until she did some work on her Adult Child of an Addict issues. Until then, Cinderella's ball couldn't have met the unrealistic expectations that she had from her family of origin. She did eventually work through these issues and after that those two special days were sane and enjoyable.

We shared before about the use of anger as a defense against anyone saying anything about an addict's usage, but it bears repeating. Addicts find that when they speak aggressively or act aggressively, the conversation usually stops concerning their addictive behaviors.

It becomes easier for the family to ignore the elephant in the living room than to try to tackle it. Meanwhile, the pile behind the elephant keeps growing and smelling worse, but everybody in the family just pinches their nose shut and pretends that it isn't happening.

The exact opposite tactic used by addicts from aggression is to be charming and funny. As one wife told me concerning her husband's drinking, "He is not a mean drunk. He is always witty and even charming and nobody else seems to mind his drinking. I sometimes wonder if I'm just a big killjoy, but I worry about him and it's not as funny for me to watch as it is for other people." Charming addicts are very difficult to confront, because after all they are, well, charming!

Now let's look at the role of the wife in this addictive family. The wife is usually the chief enabler in the system, although the children enable too as we will see later on. The wife may become super responsible and take over many of the duties that the husband should be doing. The feelings she has are usually guilt, anger and tiredness.

She may feel guilty that maybe she isn't a good enough wife, which sentiment is probably reinforced by her alcoholic husband. She may try some perfectionism of her own, thinking that if she does things extremely right then the alcoholic will have no reason to be dissatisfied and keep drinking.

I recall a wife who was going through family week that thought this very thing. She tried to be perfect and appease her alcoholic husband until she was so tired that she didn't think she could go on. Her summary statement was "I have tried so hard to please him. I thought that maybe if I had his dinner on the table at exactly 5:30 when he came home and if I fixed his favorite meals and if I had sex with him 7 nights a week instead of only 5 and if I lost some weight and if the house was always clean and if the kids didn't disturb him after he arrived and if I didn't spend any money on myself and if I kept my mother away, then he would be happy and wouldn't need to drink. But none of it has worked and I just don't care anymore."

If being perfect doesn't work, the chief enabler might go the opposite way and become very powerless and sickly. The subconscious thought here is that if she is unable to perform daily living tasks, then the alcoholic husband will have to quit drinking and pick up some of the slack. Maybe he will feel sorry for her and change his ways and help out a little bit.

Whatever strategies the spouse and chief enabler may employ, their main task is to hold everything together in the family. They may have to go back to work to support the dwindling savings because of chemical usage. They will often take over almost all responsibilities of dealing with the children, including: discipline, helping with homework, running the kids to sports and school functions and cooking and cleaning for them.

This spouse may develop a sick kind of self-importance from taking care of everything in the household. They may tell themselves that the family just can't make it without them. As one wife of an alcoholic put it, "I don't know what they would do without me"! There oftentimes is a self-righteous martyrdom that accompanies this role that is very unhealthy.

The children in a dysfunctional family system all have roles to play as well. Nobody has to tell them what role they are to play; they just seem to naturally adjust to what is going on around them and instinctively do what they can to keep the system afloat. To children, the scariest thing that they can imagine is their family breaking apart and they will sacrifice themselves to make sure that this does not happen.

The eldest child oftentimes, but not always, takes on the role of "the model child". This role has also been called the "family hero" by some experts in the field of addiction. The model child, as the title implies helps the family to look good, which distracts from the addiction problems that are going on with the parents. The task of the model child is to uphold the honor of the family. To that end, this child will be a very high achiever. He or she may excel in sports, be on the honor role, have excellent manners and be very responsible at home and in the community. Folks in the community will notice this child and comment on what a great kid this is, who is so good-natured, successful, helpful and upright. This is the young person that seems to have it all together and these achievements make up for the deficits of the parents. This child brings pride and a sense of self-worth to the family, but at a great cost.

There is a tremendous amount of pressure on the model child. After all the word, "model" has the connotation of being a cheap imitation of the real thing. The model child never gets to be a real child with all of the emotional struggles, ups and downs and teenage angst that real children must have to grow up to be healthy. To try to be good all the time and always be successful is very stressful and very tiring.

The model child cannot afford to make mistakes and learn from them. He or she just has to always do what others expect that is right and proper. Model children are very perceptive and can guess well at what other people would find appropriate or pleasing. They feel for other people, but not for themselves. They believe that they can take care of everyone, just like they do at their dysfunctional home.

I think back to a woman who was in family week many years ago. She shared that her father was an alcoholic and her mother was very sickly and just stayed in bed most of the time. She was the oldest child and said that when she was 10 years old, she got up every morning, got cleaned up and dressed, then set about to take care of her three younger siblings. She fed all of them, made sure they had clean clothes on and had their lunches packed. She walked them to the bus and waited for them when they came home. She made supper for them and then sat down to review homework with each one of them. On Saturdays she would clean the house and make meals. On Sundays she would get the kids up for Sunday School and walk them to church. In short, she did everything that her parents should have been doing but didn't, because they were too sick. She was a little adult when she should have been a kid. She grew up and married an alcoholic, because this was her version of "normal".

Another role that a sibling might have in the dysfunctional family is to be "the family foul-up". Sometimes this role is also called the family "scapegoat". This is an easier role for a child to play because it doesn't take much effort – all you have to do is screw up from time to time. The family foul-up does the opposite things of the model child. The foul-up gets failing grades, does no chores around the house, gets in trouble with the law, may use drugs, is sexually promiscuous at a young age, acts hateful and hangs around with loser friends.

It is the job of the family foul-up to give the family something to focus on other than the parent's chemical usage. This role is very reminiscent of the origin of the word, "scapegoat". In ancient times the children of Israel would take a goat and symbolically place all their sins on this goat and then drive it out into the wilderness, thus feeling free from any sin from that point on. The family foul-up is the person upon whom all the family's sins are laid. Anything that happens is blamed on this child, which, of course, takes the spotlight off the parent's chemical usage.

Even though this is an easy role to perform, because all one has to do is mess up and do nothing good, there is still a huge price that is being paid here as well. There is self-destruction, which oftentimes includes chemical dependency or other dependencies. The family foul-up obviously has a very poor self-image and feelings of rejection by others. Guilt and shame are constant companions. This child is sacrificing herself so that the family must stay together to deal with her problems. Her parents will have to talk to one another to decide what to do with her as the wayward child and thus, she is keeping them together.

If there are more children in the dysfunctional family one of them is likely to become "the invisible child". Some addiction experts also call this role the "lost child". The invisible child offers some relief to the addicted family, because she never causes any problems. She avoids stress and finds comfort in solitude. She will most likely be found in her own room reading a book or listening to her music. She will appear to her classmates as aloof and withdrawn. She keeps a low profile at all times and only answers questions in class when directly asked to do so. She has a very stunted social life and comes across as disinterested in other people and activities.

The invisible child does not seem to have much impact on keeping the family together, but she does provide some respite from the frantic nature of the rest of the family. She causes no problems and has a calming effect on the rest of the household. It appears that she is the only one who is not really affected by the dysfunction around her. This is deceiving, however, because the invisible child is immersed in loneliness. There is little connection with the family and almost no interaction with the rest of the world. This intense loneliness sometimes manifests itself in eating disorders such as anorexia, bulimia, or being overweight. There is also a kind of quiet rage that simmers inside the invisible child, because it appears that she is regarded as nothing in the family and is not even worth finding out if there is something wrong with her.

If there are enough children in the family, there might be another role and that would be "the jokester". Sometimes this role is also known as "the mascot". The jokester is oftentimes the youngest of the children. This child is usually very cute and is the kind of child that parents like to dress up and show off. The jokester loves attention and will do almost anything to create a laugh for others. It would be an interesting study for some researcher to look at comedians and find out if their background included dysfunction and if they were the family jokester even at a young age.

The function of the jokester is to provide some comic relief to a family that is weighed down by guilt and shame. This child brings some good feelings to the family and brings laughter, which relieves tension. It is hard to stand on tiptoes every minute of every day, looking out the window to see what next disaster is going to strike the family. The jokester makes sure that there is at least temporary relief from this tension by making jokes, being goofy, acting clumsy and laughing over silly things.

The jokester pays a price, however, just like all the other roles pay a price. For one thing, this child is never taken seriously. Everybody sees him as immature and this retards natural development. There is also a tremendous fear of going crazy and the anxiety of keeping a happy face creates stress and oftentimes physical illness. There is an old rock and roll song entitled "The tears of a clown" and this always reminds me of the family jokester.

In summary, all of the family roles have their part in keeping the family functioning in a very dysfunctional way. The dysfunctional family is kind of like a mobile that hangs from the ceiling. If you move one of the parts of the mobile or take one away, the whole thing tends to crash. There is a delicate balancing act that all the parts of the family have to play to keep the game going.

13
Enabling

We have used the term, "enabling" a lot in the previous chapters, but maybe it is not clear to everyone just what enabling means. Enabling is not always a dirty word. Certainly, if we have people that we care about and we try to help them succeed in various pursuits, this could be called enabling. For example, when we help our children understand their homework this is enabling them to have a better education. When we get the catcher's mitt out and let our son practice his pitching, this is enabling him to have a chance to make the team. When we show our children how to properly run the lawnmower, this enables them to take over the lawn chores.

Thus, most enabling starts out being well-motivated. When we see someone in our family or one of our close friends struggling, we will try to help them out. We don't want to see our loved ones in trouble, so we take steps to make sure that this doesn't happen. We rally around the person with a problem and help to defend them against further consequences. We pull them out of legal jams, pay off their debts, let them move back home, cover for them at work, persuade the police to just take them home instead of charging them with DUI and generally make excuses for them.

An addictive family system reminds me of several old "B" movie

Westerns that I have watched. In these shows the soldiers in the frontier fort are fighting amongst themselves and have some terrible feuds. They are about ready to kill each other. However, when the Indians show up and attack the fort, these soldiers can all seem to pull together and fight off the outside threat. This is what happens in addictive families. They may be at each other's throats and threaten all kinds of things, but when outside problems threaten, they are able to set aside their differences and take care of that threat. Then they go back to fighting with each other.

Most folks will not come to the conclusion that their loved one has an addiction, even though addiction is the most common cause of problems in families. We will look for any other reason for unreasonable behavior than addiction, because addiction has such a stigma in our culture. We don't want to think our loved one is an addict and we don't want to be related to an addict. The symptoms of addiction are nasty and we don't want to be associated with that. With the loss of values and lowering of moral standards that this spiritual disease brings, it is no wonder that families try to believe the issue is anything but addiction. As one of my recovering alcoholic friends put it, "My family didn't want to think that they were related to a cheat, a thief and a liar, because that's what I was."

Another reason that families tend to avoid seeing the obvious in their addictive loved ones is probably the same reason that families don't want to see other fatal diseases in their loved ones. For example, I talked with a family who had their husband and father in the hospital with stage 4 cancer. He had tumors all over his body and looked terrible. As we talked, the family made it clear that they were in denial over the seriousness of the patient's condition. They kept listening to the patient say that his father had a lot of fatty tumors and they turned out to be nothing, so they didn't need to get worried about his tumors.

Another family that I dealt with had a similar reaction over a case of Congestive Heart Failure. They had heard the patient talk about shortness of breath and pain in his arm and shoulder, but blew it off because he had always been "healthy as a horse". He was having a heart attack and needed surgery to save his life.

So, whenever we as family members have to think about fatal diseases, we would rather think that it is something less fatal and will talk as if it were that. Instead of looking at addiction we tend to say that it is something else like: "he is under a lot of pressure, she has always had a wild streak, he is just young and sewing his oats, he works hard and deserves to blow off a little steam" or some other excuse. Addiction is nasty and it is fatal and we would just rather not think that it is that.

Those are the reasons that enabling of addicts gets started. It almost always comes out of a desire to love and help, but can end up hindering instead and helping to kill. The following are examples of this unsuspecting enabling.

I have worked with numerous spouses who were trying to help their addicted mate by driving them to wherever they needed to go. They want them to be safe and they want them to not get DUI's so that they can keep their jobs and drive to work. But all this really does is let the addict off the hook and they don't need to worry about not drinking or using, because they know their spouse will take care of it. You can see how this kind of enabling makes sense in a sick sort of way, because if the addict loses his license, then he can't work and then the home gets repossessed and then they are out on the street. It is enabling to avert disaster. Unfortunately, these tactics rarely work for long and the feared consequences happen anyway unless there is recovery.

Recently, I talked to a set of parents who were concerned that their daughter might be depressed, because she was not doing well in school. She had dropped several classes and had flunked several more. They said they were paying for her college and at this rate it was going to take her 10 years to get enough credits to graduate and they weren't sure they could afford this. When I began to ask them questions about chemical usage, they tried to deflect these questions and make excuses for their daughter. They said they did find a whiskey bottle in her sock drawer when she came home for Fall Break, but they minimized this as being normal college experimentation. The more questions I asked, the more convinced I was that this young woman's problem was not depression, but alcohol. These were good people with good hearts and good intentions, but they were unwittingly enabling their daughter to drink and blow off classes.

Another set of parents that I talked to were upset with the legal system because they had gotten in trouble for supplying their teenage son and his friends with liquor. They told me the story of how they had seen their son come home intoxicated on several occasions and were worried that he might wreck the car or be in a wreck in one of his friend's cars. They thought that it would be much safer for all the kids if they would just have them come to their home and they would supply the liquor and then drive those teens home. Although these parents viewed their actions as helpful, I saw them as enabling behaviors. Not only was what they were doing illegal, but it was not helpful.

It is not unusual at all for spouses of addicts to make regular calls in to employers to tell them that the addict is sick and cannot make it in to work today. Sometimes they will even get Doctor's excuses for their addicted loved one to make sure the boss doesn't think that they are just faking it.

There have been countless stories over the years that I have worked with addictions about family members bailing loved ones out of jail. Usually the thought of abuse and prison rape are enough to send family members running to the bail bondsman to make sure that their child or spouse does not get permanently damaged.

Although enabling almost always starts out with innocence and ignorance, as the reality grows that this problem really is an addiction, the enabling behaviors get more and more unhealthy and unreasonable.

For example, there was a mother that I talked to some years ago who was in the hospital for ulcers and a general nervous condition. As we explored what some of her stressors were in life, she eventually began telling me about her son, who lived with her. She kept talking about her "little boy" and how unlucky he was and how needy he was. Eventually I asked just how old this little boy was and she told me that he was thirty-two! She said that he had lost his job about 7 years ago and could not seem to find the right kind of work that he liked. He had been living with her all of his life and had only moved out for a few months when he was 25. She paid for all of his food and living expenses. She had bought him a car and paid the insurance on that. She said that she knew that he had a problem with alcohol, but she didn't want him to get into trouble with the law, so she stopped and bought him a bottle of whiskey every day so that he wouldn't get caught driving drunk.

When I suggested that maybe she was making it a bit too easy for him to keep drinking, she got rather huffy with me and said that she wasn't one of those mothers who abandoned their children, just because they ran into a little trouble. She followed that up by asking, "Where would he go without me? How would he live"? From her defensiveness, it did not appear that her little boy was ever going to get a chance to find out. This mother's reactions were well beyond being just an unwitting accomplice to her son's disease; she was an active participant in helping to keep him sick with this kind of desperate enabling. Her son had no need to change what he was doing, because there were no consequences for it. Why should he change? At the end of our conversation I shifted my tactics a bit and tried to engage this woman with some teasing, which actually worked better. I said, "Have you ever considered adopting an aging Lutheran chaplain? I think if you would just do that I would have it made"!

Another set of parents that I remember were almost all the way down the rabbit hole of enabling by the time I met them. They had a son that was hooked on cocaine and anything else he could get his hands on. He was in his late 20's and was living with them. They paid all his expenses for everything and decided that if they gave him a drug allowance, then he wouldn't have to rob a gas station like his friends had done and wouldn't get into legal trouble. They kept giving him his drug allowance until they had used up all their savings. They next dipped into their 401K fund until that was all gone. Then they started noticing that items were missing from their house and knew their son was selling these items for drugs as well. They also shared that one thing that really bothered them was that even when they were in the house, they had to lock their purse and wallet in the safe at all times, because otherwise their son was in there taking all their cash and their credit cards.

In short, these people were captives in their own home. They were enabling in the worst way and were too intimidated not to keep doing so. Their son was a big brute of a man and definitely had an intimidating presence and manner. Both of these parents were starting to experience physical ailments due solely to stress.

For any of us who care about a person with the disease of addiction, it is hard not to do a certain amount of enabling at first, because we care. But addiction is a disease that requires a certain degree of pain and suffering for the addict in order for them to get well. There is an old saying that we have all heard that says, "If it ain't broke, don't fix it". This is the premise under which addicts operate. Until it is very clear that something is broken, nothing will change. Until the addict has been confronted with the reality that things are broken because of his sickness, nothing gets fixed. There are broken promises, broken furniture, broken bank accounts and broken hearts. This needs to be made clear.

The phrase, "It's not that bad", comes into play often for not only addicts, but their families and friends. But if one asks that question the other way around, it sounds fairly ridiculous. "So, it's not that bad. How bad do you want it to get"? "Do you want it to be bad, really bad or fatally bad"? That's not the right question. The question we should be asking about our lives is how good they could be, not how bad they have to be before we change.

In actuality, it is not just addicted persons that have to have things go badly before they change – everybody seems to operate on this system. For example, when do we go on a diet? When swimsuit season is upon us and/or we can't get into any of our clothes. When do students start studying? When the test is the next day and they might be failing. When do we go to see a Doctor? We go when the pain in our leg gets so bad that we can't walk. When do we start looking for a new job? We start when we begin having dreams that we don't have to go to work where we are anymore.

Likewise, addicted persons don't just wake up one morning and say, "Well, everything seems to be going just swell in my life, so I think I'll drop in at the local treatment center and get some help." Don't count on that. It is only when the pain of life as is becomes worse than the fear of the unknown that people get help from addictions. Addicts need their pain and it is the only friend they have when it comes to being willing to get help.

That is the reason why enabling, whether unwitting or desperate delays treatment for people who need it. On an average, enablers usually delay treatment for those they love at least 10 years and unfortunately, many die before they ever get to that 10 year deadline.

One way to view enabling is to picture one person falling all over the place, while his friend keeps throwing big pillows down in front of him. The man who is doing the falling is not going to worry too much about falling, because he knows he won't get hurt; someone is always going to be there to bail him out with the pillows. Similarly, it is only when we metaphorically let the addict hit the pavement with his nose a few times that he realizes that the sidewalk is hard and maybe he should do something to change his flopping behavior.

But we don't just let the addict keep falling for nothing. We use these painful experiences to nudge the addict towards help. We don't wait until the addict has "hit bottom" and lost everything before we intervene. Too many addicts are dead before that happens. We use their pain to bring the bottom up to hit them and make them realize they need help. We will explain this process more in the chapter on intervention.

For those of us who have addicts that we care about, it is a delicate balancing act when we try to be helpful. The two extremes look to be the only options that we have. The one extreme is to be so sucked in to the addict's denial system and to our own denial that we simply keep enabling them and making it easier for them to keep the addictive behavior going. The other extreme is to simply get fed up with the lies, the selfishness, the hurt and the disappointment and totally abandon the addict. We are tempted to wash our hands of them and have no contact whatsoever from this point on.

I talked to a brother of an alcoholic recently that said that he had in fact, abandoned his sick brother. He said, "I am done with him. He has lied to me for the last time. I don't talk to him. I don't accept calls from him. I don't listen to him. I don't want to know where he is and what he's doing. He is dead to me."

But somewhere in between those two extremes of enabling and abandoning lies mental health. To not only be useful to the addict that we care about, but to become healthy ourselves, we must find a way to emotionally detach from the addict without abandoning. This is not an easy thing to do, but gets much easier when we do it with other people who are in codependent positions. The fellowship of Alanon is where most folks learn to successfully detach without abandoning.

When we learn how to detach, it doesn't mean that we don't care anymore about the addict, it just means that we remove ourselves from the problem. When our addicted friend comes to us needing money for rent, because he used his paycheck on cocaine, we say, "That is a tough situation. I don't know how you are going to do that. I'm not going to bail you out anymore, because I don't like spending my money on cocaine, but rest assured that I will be there for you when you go to treatment". We stop making excuses for them, stop calling in sick for them, stop giving them money, stop doing their jobs for them and stop yelling at them. We just let the natural consequences of their actions push them ever closer to feeling enough pain to want to get help. Sometimes we can even enhance that pain to move them a little more quickly towards recovery.

In summary, enabling may start out as being helpful and a friend, but actually winds up assisting the disease to continue. Usually, when enabling ceases, the addict reaches out for help and then we can really be of some help in their treatment and recovery.

14

Diagnosing Addiction

As we stated in an earlier chapter, it is not always easy to determine what is regular, social using of addictive agents and what is pathological, unhealthy, out-of-control using. If you are not an addiction specialist it is even harder to decipher what would be considered a problem and what would not.

For the addicted person themselves, this is never an issue, because they never believe that they have a problem until it is so obvious to everybody that they can't deny it. And even then they will still try to deny it.

If I am an addicted person, my thinking is that the person that really has a problem with drugs, alcohol or some other addictive agent is the person whose using is a little different from mine. So, if I drink beer, then the guy who has a problem is the guy who drinks whiskey. If I drink whiskey, the gal with a problem is the gal who drinks whiskey every day. If I drink whiskey every day, the guy with the real problem is the guy who uses Oxycontin. If I use Oxycontin, the guy with a problem is the guy who uses street drugs like heroin every day. You can see how this kind of delusional thinking goes. A problem is any pattern of using that is not like mine!

There are some standard questions that are found in addiction diagnostic questionnaires that are very helpful to keep in mind if you are wondering about your own using habits or more likely, if you are looking at someone else's habits.

One clear sign that drinking and using are getting out of control is if a person experiences increased tolerance of the addictive agent. If it takes more alcohol, more pills or more of anything to get the person high, that is a sign that your body is getting used to using and it will take more of the substance to get the same effect. The irony of this is that in our culture, being able to hold your liquor or smoke a fatty is seen as some kind of badge of honor. The reality is that this increased tolerance is not some twisted sign of being a real man, but only means that you are getting sicker. Your body is getting used to having more toxins and poisons in it. And if you don't have these toxins present in your system, your cells will rebel. This is what withdrawal symptoms are; a reaction to not having the addictive agents present in your system. Even having a hangover after excessive drinking is a mild version of withdrawal symptoms.

I can recall a classmate of mine in High School whose sole claim to fame was that he could drink more beer than anybody else in our class. He wasn't very athletic, wasn't talented musically and wasn't a great student. However, he did attain a sick kind of status in our adolescent world because of his increased tolerance with alcohol. Not coincidentally, he ended up becoming an alcoholic and was killed in a car accident while driving drunk. We were all shocked, but we certainly should have seen that one coming.

Another diagnostic sign of addiction is the use of addictive agents for relief or like a medicine. If you use drinking or pills to get to sleep and stay asleep and do this consistently, you are headed for trouble. If you drink or take other drugs to relieve physical pain and these are not prescribed for you, it could mean trouble. If you are nervous without some chemical on board, that is not a good sign. If you can't seem to interact socially or have a good time without drinking or using something, it could well be a problem.

Solitary usage indicates an incipient problem as well. Drinking alone and drinking to get drunk is not a very social way to drink. Sitting alone at a bar and downing several drinks before going home is not healthy. Smoking pot all alone and just sitting there and zoning out is not helpful.

Having a stash to make sure you always have something on hand to take the edge off is not a good sign. If you are hiding a bottle or making sure that you have the second bottle just in case the first one runs out, this shows your growing dependency. I can recall a couple good stories from former clients that illustrate this.

One man who was in his late 40's was a pretty late stage alcoholic and his codependent wife was really into control to make sure that he wasn't drinking too much. He went out to the back yard to do a little sunbathing one Saturday and the wife felt secure for a little bit because she could keep an eye on him from the kitchen window. He took no bottle with him, so she felt relief that maybe they could have a good day. However, after a few hours her husband came back into the house and he was knee-walking, pant-peeing drunk. She could not figure out how he did it, because she had her eye on him the whole time. When he finally came in for treatment, he confessed to his group that he had taken his whiskey bottle out at night and had buried it in the yard with a straw sticking out of a cork from it. He placed his towel so that his head would be even with the straw and as he lay on his stomach, he was pulling on that straw all afternoon!

Another patient that I remember was doing some repair work on the roof of his house. His wife was also into control and made sure he couldn't drink by going up the ladder and looking around on the roof. She was baffled because every time he got done roofing, he would weave down the ladder "drunk as a skunk". He later admitted that he had taken a huge bottle of whiskey up the ladder before he started the roofing project and had tied twine around it and then tied the twine around the chimney and lowered the bottle down inside the chimney where it would not be seen by his wife's inspection of the roof. That certainly isn't exactly social drinking either!

Another sign of a growing addiction is unplanned using. This might include: stopping for a few drinks when you had not intended to, drinking more than you had set out to drink and being the last one to leave the party when you had planned to get home early. There is a sensation that addicts talk about that lets them experience being out of control. It is when they start using and then it seems like one hand is drinking and the other hand is ordering another one. One hand is smoking and the other hand is rolling the next joint. One pill is downed and the other hand is pouring out two more pills. It is described as if that second hand has taken on a life of its own and is not connected to the body. I read some Oriental wisdom that speaks to this phenomenon. It goes like this: "First the man takes a drink. Then the drink takes a drink. Then the drink takes the man". It is the sensation of the second part of this saying when the drink takes a drink that we are talking about. There is the automatic reaction to use more. The person didn't really decide to have more - they just had more.

A real clue that drinking alcohol is out of control is when a person experiences blackouts. A blackout is a loss of memory from drinking excessively. This is not the same as passing out. Passing out is when the mind and the body both crash and there is unconsciousness. Blacking out is when a person's body keeps moving, their mouth keeps talking and they are still upright and doing things, but their brain is not recording what they are doing. It is a period of amnesia caused by prolonged overload of alcohol on the brain.

Sometimes alcoholics will try to use blackouts as excuses for inappropriate behavior. When confronted with what they did and said from the night before, many an alcoholic has responded with," I can't believe I did that. I don't remember that"! However, other people don't take this excuse as a very good one. They tend to believe that even if your brain wasn't recording what you did, you still did it and it all counts.

I saw a funny joke about this some years ago and it might have been in the A.A. Grapevine magazine. It told of two men getting ready to fight a duel with each other with pistols at twenty paces. One man was a huge person and the other was a very skinny person. The wide man thought that it wasn't fair that he had such a thin target to aim at and the other had a huge target. The thin man suggested that he back up another 10 paces so that he had further to shoot. The wide man recognized that he would also have further to shoot at the thin target and vetoed this idea. Finally, the thin man, who was a schoolteacher, took a stick of chalk out of his suit pocket and drew two lines about a foot apart down the middle of the wide man's dark vest. Then the thin man said, "There, now any shots outside of those two lines don't count"! That excuse doesn't seem to cut much ice with those who are hurt by an addict's behavior. They don't care if he was in a blackout or not. They think all the shots count!

Sometimes a blackout is only a memory loss for a short period of time. Oftentimes a blackout means a loss of memory after a certain amount of drinking the night before. But there are some blackouts that are extraordinary. The most bizarre blackout that was ever related to me was by an alcoholic in treatment. He said that he had started drinking in Indianapolis on a Friday, but when he came out of the blackout, it was Tuesday and he did not recognize his surroundings. He looked around and found out that he was in San Francisco. But he also had receipts from meals and rooms that he had purchased in Dallas and Denver as well! He had apparently gotten drunk and just kept on drinking for days and never came out of the blackout until 4 days later. He had no idea who he had talked to or what he had done. He hadn't wound up in jail, so he reasoned that he must have behaved himself, even while drunk.

Blackouts are scary to alcoholics, because they will never know exactly what they have done or said and suspect it could have been bad. Any person who has had blackouts can never say, "I would never..." because they simply don't know. There is some free-floating anxiety and guilt over what might have happened, but no way of knowing.

Another diagnostic sign of addiction is "warm-ups". This technique is used by addicts when they know that there is going to be drinking or drug usage at a party, but they fear that it might be too tame a social event and they might not get enough of their favorite drug to get a good buzz. So, the solution to this is to have some warm-up drinks or drugs before the party, so that the party can then finish off a good high. Nobody will think that they have a problem, because they were only using moderately as everybody else and if they act loaded, the others will just think they don't have a very high tolerance.

Related to warm-ups is the tendency to gulp drinks or pills. If a person orders a double right away and downs that hurriedly and then orders or fixes another right away, this is another technique to make sure that the drug intake will be enough to get high. For an addict, if there is not enough booze or drugs to get high, there is really no point in starting. In fact, it is very irritating to just use a little bit, but not enough to really feel it. Most addicted persons won't even start using if they don't think they can finish it off with a good high. They realize that to start using sets in motion the phenomenon of craving and they will have to find a way to finish it off or be horribly frustrated.

There is a phrase that alcoholics have used for a long time to describe a remedy for the withdrawal symptoms of a hangover and that phrase is "the hair of the dog that bit you". This quaint expression really points out a very serious symptom of problem using and that is the morning drink or the morning pill. People with drug/alcohol problems usually find out that they can stave off the withdrawal symptoms simply by never completely sobering up. The morning drink can stop the morning tremors or "shakes", but it is a real diagnostic sign that there is a problem.

A shorthand way of thinking about a diagnosis of dependency for another person is to think in terms of the three P's, which stands for preoccupation, purpose and pattern. If you have someone that you suspect has an addiction problem or if it is even you yourself that you are concerned about, considering these three phenomena will give you a clearer picture.

The first concern is does the person seem to be preoccupied with drinking and using? Do they think about using when they should be thinking about almost anything else? Do they make plans to use and find ways to justify the using in case anybody else wonders about it? Do they look forward to the end of the day so that they can drink or use? Do they make big plans for the weekend that involve using? Is there a particular time of the day that they feel a need for a drink? This business of craving at a certain time of the day is very prevalent in tobacco addiction, for example. There are certain times of every day that smokers and chewers always think about using. These times are: first thing in the morning, with coffee at breakfast, at morning break time at work, after every meal, at afternoon break time, every time they get into a car, and before bed. Other cigarettes are smoked in between these expected times to fill in as well.

The second concern would be if the person you are concerned about seems to be drinking, smoking or using with a purpose. That purpose might be to deal with stress at work or at home. It might be to try to deal with grief and loss issues. It might be to be able to be sociable and relax. It might be in order to sleep or stay asleep. If there appears to be a real purpose to the using, it usually means trouble.

The third concern would be to look at a person's using pattern. Is the pattern showing a very heavy concentration of using? Is there any change in the pattern? For example, has the person switched from beer to whiskey? Have they started only going to those functions where they know there will be drinking or drugging? Have they started having several drinks after work instead of just one? Do they justify their using more than ever before? Did they used to just drink on the weekends, but now the weekend seems to start on Wednesday and ends up on Tuesday?

Another way of diagnosing addiction and probably the most reliable method, is what we mentioned in Chapter One and will now explain in greater detail, namely, to look at the problems the using has caused. There are five major areas in a person's life that problems may show up in from chemical usage: relationships, health, legal, financial and job/school. If addictive agents cause any problems in any one of these areas of life, it is a problem. You don't have to have problems in all five areas for the using to be considered a problem and if you do see problems in all five areas it almost always means that the person is not only addicted, but in a very late stage of the addiction.

Let's look at this from the viewpoint of someone who is wondering if their using might be a problem. If drinking, smoking, using, gambling or any other behavior is a concern to other people who care about you, there is almost certainly reason to be concerned. Other people don't care if you drink or use as long as it doesn't cause any problems. It is only when they start to notice that your using is negatively affecting others and yourself that they get concerned. The simplest way to express this is by saying "that which causes problems is a problem and that which never causes any problems is not a problem".

A good example of this kind of assessment is my two grandfathers. As stated in the chapter on ACOA's my maternal grandfather was a chronic alcoholic. However, my paternal grandfather was a drinker as well. In fact, Grandpa John drank almost every day of his life, but he was not an alcoholic. What's the difference? Grandpa John's drinking never caused any problems in his life. Every day for supper after farming all day he would have a beer as the beverage with his supper. It was kind of a European style of drinking where the beer was his beverage with the meal. He did not follow this beer up with 14 more or even 2 or 3 more. He just had one beer with his meal. He sometimes had 2 or 3 beers over the course of an afternoon when he was playing cards with his four sons at a family get-together, but he never got drunk and never got into trouble. That is what the term "social drinking" means. A person drinks with others to have a good time and nothing bad ever comes of it. As soon as something bad results it's not very social, it's a problem.

So, if your wife suggests that you cut back on your drinking, she probably has a good reason for wanting you to do that. Either she is concerned about your health or she doesn't like the way you talk to her when drinking or the way you ignore her when drinking. If your husband doesn't want to take you to his company picnic and says it is because you are always so zoned out on pot and it is embarrassing to him to even introduce you to other people, you can be sure your smoking is a problem. If your friends no longer want to go out to supper with you because they tell you that you always drink too much and start berating them and being rude to them, you can be sure that the drinking is a problem. If your co-workers won't lend you money because you have gambled it away before, that's a problem.

One bizarre example of other people being concerned about one's drug use was related to me by a great friend of mine who has been in recovery from his addiction for 35 years. He said that when he was a young man he used to spend his winters in the Bahamas. He said getting marijuana in the Bahamas was as easy as finding corn in Indiana. He was smoking his brains out every day with the Rastafarians. He said that finally some of these folks sat him down and had a little kind of intervention with him and told him, "you are smoking too much of the gange, man". My friend concluded that when the Rastafarians are saying that you are smoking too much dope, you might just have a problem!

Another relationship that always seems to suffer if there is a growing addiction is the relationship with a person's Higher Power. Excessive using of addictive agents causes guilt and guilt always causes distance and separation in relationships. When we feel guilty the last person we want to run into is the person or Being about whom we feel most guilty. For example, if my neighbor had asked me to drop off his income tax payment in the mail, because I was going to the Post Office anyway and if I threw that envelope in the back seat and forget to mail it, there will be repercussions. Later on when the G-men come and haul my neighbor away and after he gets done with his prison term for non-payment of taxes, I am not going to be very comfortable with running into him. If I see him walking down the sidewalk towards me, I am going to turn on my heel and walk the other way. That's what guilt does to relationships. And that is what happens to our relationship with our Higher Power or our God, however we understand God. That is why addiction is the ultimate escape from God and why recovery is a spiritual process that repairs that relationship by dealing with the guilt.

Problems in relationships of all sorts are usually the first problems that show up in addiction. Even if problems have not yet occurred in other areas, the first and most important area to look at would be problems in relationship to others.

The second major area that could incur problems from addiction is in the area of finances. Depending upon which drug or addictive agent you are using, it might not be long before you will have difficulty keeping up with the cost. If you are using alcohol and have a decent job, you may be able to withstand the cost. However, if you are using something like cocaine or heroin, a regular job cannot cover that amount of money spent on drugs. Unless you are independently wealthy, there are only about three ways to keep up with a crack habit, for example. You can engage in either dealing, stealing or prostituting or maybe all three. If you are a male you are probably limited to just dealing and stealing realistically to make ends meet.

Sometimes the financial hardship alerts others that there could be a problem with an addiction. For instance, when a family loses their house or car through repossession, but both parents are working at decent jobs, it is most likely either addiction or catastrophic medical bills with no health insurance.

For something like a gambling addiction, this area of problems with finances will show up very early and usually at about the same time as problems in relationships. Since money is part of the addictive agent of gambling, invariably there will be gambling loss and then the fights start at home over not having enough money to cover the bills.

There is also a sick connection between a gambling addiction and an addiction to drugs or alcohol. The symbiotic relationship between these addictions goes like the following. When you drink excessively, you knock out the inhibitory center of the brain and you get more daring with your gambling. When you gamble more you either win, in which case you celebrate with more drinking, or you lose, in which case you feel you must drown your sorrows with more drinking. When you do more drinking, you get even more reckless and you again either win or lose, in which case more drinking ensues. Eventually, every gambler loses, because the odds favor the house. The result is a combined problem with both drinking and gambling or drugs and gambling.

Sometimes money wasted on drugs or other addictions is the sole reason that people want to quit. An example of this is my father. He began smoking tobacco at age 20 at the beginning of World War II, at a time when many people smoked and nobody really knew how bad it was for your health. He eventually knew that smoking was bad for his health, but was addicted to tobacco and didn't want to quit. However, he had said that if cigarettes ever went up to 75 cents per pack, he was going to have to quit. His exact quote was "I can't raise enough cattle to keep up with prices like that". Of course it didn't take long and cigarettes were over 75 cents per pack and that is when he quit. The financial pinch was all it took for him to give the tobacco up. But as Nicotine Dependency Counselor for the hospital I certainly know that it takes a lot more problems than that for most folks to quit tobacco. Usually it also takes health issues.

Incurring legal difficulties is the third area to consider when diagnosing addiction. One of the most common problems caused by addictions in this area is the DUI charge for folks driving under the influence. It is possible for a social drinker to be careless at say, his brother's wedding and drink too much and get picked up for a DUI. However, if somebody gets a second DUI or a third or more, to me that is an automatic sign of addiction. You are either in love with the judge or you are an addict!

There can be any number of other legal problems from addictions as well. If a person has a drunk and disorderly, reckless endangerment, possession of a controlled substance, or distribution of drugs charge, these are real red flags for addiction also. Sometimes even things that don't seem directly related such as non-payment of child support are actually caused by addiction.

The fourth major area of life that could show an addiction problem is in the area of physical or mental health. Everybody knows that alcohol consumption is hard on the liver, but there are many other physical signs that alcohol might be a problem. Alcoholics have about 4 times as many heart attacks and strokes as the average person. There are other things like esophageal bleeding that are from excessive drinking more often than not. Various gastrointestinal complaints are common among drinkers.

If we look at other addictive agents, there are health problems consistent with these substances too. Cocaine users often have nasal injuries from snorting coke. Methamphetamine users usually have rotted teeth after extensive usage. Tobacco users have breathing problems and heart problems many times. Food addicts have tremendous weight gain from overeating or eroded teeth from bulimia with binging and purging. Heroin users may have injection site infections and blasted veins.

When we look at mental health issues, it is always a good idea to think addiction first and rule that out before any other kind of mental or emotional problem. For example, many people go to their physician or even to a mental health counselor for depression. But if there is some searching done, it is often found out that they are depressed because they are taking massive quantities of a central nervous system depressant like alcohol. Naturally, they are going to be depressed with a depressant drug on board! That is why it is imperative to rule out addiction first before going any other direction in therapy. Addiction, as we said before, is a primary disease and if this is not addressed, it doesn't really matter what kind of help is attempted, because it won't work.

The fifth major area of life where problems from addiction might show up is in the area of work or school. This is not always the last place where problems occur, but it is usually the last place. There are two reasons why addicted persons will doggedly hang onto a job, even after they have lost almost everything else in their life. The first reason is because, as we said before, it takes a lot of money to keep up with a drug habit or even an alcohol habit. An addict needs to keep their job to make sure that they have a stream of income to keep the drugs coming.

However, just as important as it is to have income to support the habit is the second reason to concentrate on the job, namely, to stay in denial that using is a problem. Maintaining a job is the best reason that an addict has to convince other people and themselves that their using can't be a problem. I can't tell you the number of times that family members have told me that they are not sure that their loved one has a problem with drugs or alcohol because "they go to work every day".

Early in my career as an addiction counselor I had an experience with an alcoholic that gave me a perspective on addicts and work that I never forgot. I was doing a DUI evaluation for the State of North Dakota on a man we will call Joe (not his real name). Joe had just gotten his third DUI and had to have an evaluation to see if he could get his driver's license back or if he required treatment first.

Joe was a pretty late stage alcoholic. I wouldn't have really had to do a very thorough assessment on him to know if he was an alcoholic. I probably could have done "the light test" on him. The light test is when you turn off the lights and watch the alcoholic's nose glow red in the dark! Joe had the kind of red-nosed, broken veins in his face of the chronic tippler. If you combine that with multiple legal problems, it didn't take long to see that he was in trouble with alcohol and would need treatment.

As I quizzed Joe on the various areas of his life that had been affected by his drinking, it included everything except his job. His wife had divorced him 15 years ago and his kids wanted nothing to do with him. He had some minor health problems consistent with alcoholism. He was living from paycheck to paycheck. Of course, he had the legal problems with the DUI's.

Finally, when I got to the area of possible work problems caused by drinking I asked him if he had had any problems getting to work or staying at work. He worked at a sand and gravel company running a pay loader that loaded up the dump trucks. His reply was "No, I always get to work on time and I've never missed a day's work in my life." I asked if he would sign a release so that I could talk to his employer and he readily agreed to this. I called his boss and asked if Joe had ever had any absenteeism or problems on the job from drinking. His boss said, "You know, it is the craziest thing. We have never had an employee like Joe before. He has worked here with us for over 13 years and in all that time he has never been absent one day that he was scheduled to work".

I was surprised at this, because I figured everybody misses a day now and again with the flu or a cold or something. I said, "Joe, your boss confirmed what you said about your perfect work attendance, but I am curious, don't you ever get the flu and end up puking and missing work"? Joe replied, "Well, how would I know"? "What", I said, unclear of his meaning? "How would I know if I had the flu? I would just puke and go to work like I do every morning"!

It dawned on me then and I have never forgotten the kind of courage that addicts display to try to keep the game going. Here was a man who was getting up every weekday morning and vomiting and going off to work with a head so big he could hardly jam it through the door, but he was going, because he needed the money to drink and he needed his best reason why his drinking was not a problem, which is "But I go to work every day".

Many times I have seen men and women lose their families, but they won't lose their jobs. They will lose their health, but will still drag themselves to their jobs. They will lose their driver's license and keep going to work on a bicycle or even a John Deere tractor and still keep their job. As one addict told me, "Wives come and go, but a good job is hard to find"!

So, the best determiner as to whether something is a problem or not is simply to see if it has ever caused any problems. It doesn't have to cause a problem every time either; it just has to cause problems sometimes to be a problem. No addicted persons get into trouble of some kind every time they use - they just never know.

I have used a visual demonstration with patients in treatment to display what this might look like. Imagine that one "x" represents one episode of chemical usage where nothing bad happens. Then imagine that one "?" represents one episode of using where something damaging happened. This is what it would look like.

SOCIAL USING xxxxxxxxxxxxxxxxxxxxxxxxxxxxxxxxxxxxxxxxxxx

xxxxxxxxxxxxxxxxxxxxxxxxxxxxxxxxxxxxxxxxxxxxxxxxxxxxxxxxxxxx
xxxxxxxxx etc.

FANTASY OF ADDICTION
???
?????????????????????? etc.

REALITY OF ADDICTION
xxxxxxxxxxxxxxxxxxxxxxxxxxxxxxxxxxxx?x?xxxxxxxxxxxx?xxxxxxx
xx??xxxxxx?xxxxx?xxxxxxxxxxx??xxxxxx?xxxxx?xxxxxxxxx???etc.

Social using would be described by the word, "never". A person may or may not drink or use some other addictive agent, but it never causes any problems in any major area of their life. If it starts to cause problems, then it is not very social. Going to jail is not my idea of a social event. Getting kicked out of the house for being obnoxiously drunk is not a social thing. Losing friends because of drunken, angry fights does not fit the definition of social.

The general public's fantasy of addiction in the second column is that an addict is somebody who drinks or uses every day and every time when they use, something tragic happens. This simply is not true. Even the most chronically addicted persons I have ever worked with don't get in trouble every time they use. They get into trouble most of the time in late stage addiction, but certainly not always. That is why when they are confronted by family members who say, "You're always drunk or you're always high", they can say with a clear conscience, "That's not true; there were a couple days just last month when I wasn't loaded"! It doesn't always happen, just most of the time.

The reality of addiction is shown in the third column. A person may go along for quite some time without experiencing any negative consequences from their using. If they ever do experience one problem, they change their behavior and it never happens again. However, the addicted person experiences a problem and vows that it will never happen again, but it does happen again and then later on, again. Thus, the reality of addiction is described by the word, "sometimes". Sometimes when that person uses, they use more than they had intended and sometimes when that happens, bad things occur in their life. It is not all the time - just sometimes, but sometimes is too much. Sometimes is kind of like putting one bullet into a pistol and then spinning the cylinder and putting the gun to your head and continuously pulling the trigger. Would you say that it was alright because it only goes off "sometimes"? No, sometimes is too much. It should be never.

A good example of diagnosing addiction from the standpoint of problems happening "sometimes" is a man that came to me many years ago for a DUI evaluation. He had a drinking pattern that was very much binge drinking with long periods of abstinence in between. He would start drinking on a Friday evening, drink all weekend, then sober up and go back to work on Monday.

He drank on only 7 weekends that year with nothing in between. His total consumption of alcohol for the year was very low and this was confirmed by his ex-wife and a friend. But I diagnosed him as an alcoholic needing treatment. The reason is because although he did not drink very often, when he did, he sometimes got in trouble in the major areas of his life. In fact, most times he got in trouble, but not always. In January of that year he rolled his truck while drunk, but wasn't charged because he was near a friend's house, who took him in and sobered him up before the police found his vehicle. In March he tossed his wife around the room and she told him she would divorce him if he ever did that again. In May he got his first DUI. He got drunk in June over one weekend but nothing happened. In August he abused his wife again and she did leave him and divorced him. In October he got a second DUI. In December he got drunk again, but nothing bad happened.

Even though he had only been drinking on 7 weekends in a year, he still was diagnosed as being alcoholic, because it is not how much someone drinks or even how often, but what problems it caused. This man's drinking caused problems not every time, but sometimes and sometimes is too much.

In the fellowship of Alcoholics Anonymous there is a saying about diagnosing when somebody becomes addicted. It goes like this: When you put a cucumber in the brine it is not always easy to say exactly when it changes, but at some point you can see that it is pickled. For addicts that point is generally whenever problems start occurring because of using.

15

Intervention

If it is true (and it is) that enabling does not help an addicted person, then what does? As we said before, pain is the thing that seems to make more humans make changes in their lives than anything else. As we said, nobody, including addicts, ever changes anything when things are going swimmingly well. We only change when it is too uncomfortable not to change. No addicted person ever woke up in the morning and said, "Well, things are going so well in my life that I think I'll drop in to a treatment center and get a little treatment"! That never happens. Statements from addicts before going into treatment sound more like this: "I can't go on anymore. I've got to do something. I have got to get some help. I give up".

There are times when people who care about addicts can actually help them into recovery by appearing to make things worse. These actions can all be called interventions. There are many different ways to intervene on an addict and they have various levels of success, but all of them are better than doing nothing and watching the addicted person die a slow, painful and unnecessary death.

There is the notion out there in the general public that nothing can be done to help addicts get help until they want help. The statements that all professionals who work with addictions have heard all sound very hopeless. For example, "You can't do anything with a drug addict until they have hit bottom". Another example is, "You can lead a horse to water, but you can't make him drink and you can't make him not drink either". "An addict has to want help or you are just wasting your time", is another opinion that I have heard many times.

But the concept of intervention is to not stand around and wait until an addict hits bottom, but rather to create a crisis that will make bottom come up until it hits them! We don't have to wait until an addicted person has lost everything, because all too often that means that they have also lost their life. Many addicts can have a relatively high bottom if that bottom is maneuvered so that it hits them earlier in their using career.

A good example of this high bottom is the seminary professor that I wrote about in the first chapter, the Rev. Dr. Duane Mehl. He started his addiction with a ruptured disc in his back for which he was taking pain medications. When his Dr. cut him off the narcotics, he switched quickly to alcohol and was drinking a bottle of wine every day. His bottom came when he drank his bottle of wine and then cracked open the second bottle, which he always kept in reserve. He got drunk and missed his classes and he was the teacher! He had some good friends who talked to him about the problem that they saw in this and that was all it took for him to get into treatment and be in continuous recovery. Their intervention at a time of crisis put him over the top. He didn't lose his job. He didn't lose his marriage. His health was still relatively intact and he was not bankrupt. But the thought of letting his students and colleagues down was enough to propel him into treatment and recovery. That is a pretty high bottom, but others could experience something similar with the proper intervention by those who care.

Sometimes concerned persons can intervene by legal methods. I can think of several spouses over the years that actually called the police or highway patrol to alert them to where their addicted loved one could be found driving under the influence of alcohol or drugs. This will almost certainly be viewed as betrayal by the addict in the family and maybe by others as well, but it is a way to create a crisis that could push the addict into treatment. In most of these cases the spouse of the addict followed up by talking to the judge before the trial and begging that judge to help the addict by mandating treatment as part of the sentence. Judges are very sympathetic to this approach most of the time and very few judges are simply vindictive.

Another legal approach may be needed if the addict doesn't drive drunk or get into other legal scrapes. Concerned persons can also file a petition for a mental health hearing with the hope that treatment would be mandated by the judge. This procedure entails going to the county Clerk of Court and filling out a petition for a mental health hearing that details the problem the addict has. Basically, there needs to be evidence of one or the other of two things. There needs to be evidence that the person is dangerous to themselves (suicidal) or is dangerous to other people (homicidal). It takes more than just hearsay for a judge to commit somebody to treatment, otherwise anybody could get anybody committed for any reason. There must be either physician's statements that indicate danger or legal documents that show dangerous past and current behaviors or corroboration from other witnesses to dangerous behaviors. This procedure sounds rather difficult, but it is actually not that involved and has worked many times to get addicts help.

A different angle to get help for an addict is to go through their employer. This seems like a very risky proposition for most family members, because there is the possibility that the addict might just be fired. This is not very likely today, because most employers are much more enlightened about behavioral health issues than they were a few decades ago. As we said in a previous chapter, the job is the most precious thing that most addicts have and they will hang onto it at all costs, so if this is threatened, addicts take it very seriously. When an employer confronts the addict with the choice of either getting help or losing their job, the vast majority of addicts will choose treatment. This is what I refer to as "the Godfather offer". It is stated much more nicely than this, but what the addict hears is this, "Do you like your job? Well then you'll love treatment". After the imaginary gun-to-the-head Godfather offer is made, it is surprising the percentage of addicts that suddenly "volunteer" to go get help.

Yet another source of helpful intervention can come from the medical profession. Many addicted persons have a very high regard for their family physician and will actually listen to them when they are told that they need to give up their drugs of one kind or another. When a physician has a good relationship and the patient knows that they are cared for and not judged, it can go a long way to that patient finally acquiescing and going for help.

This seems to work particularly well with older patients who have a long and good relationship with their physician. The older generation seems to naturally have more respect and trust in their Doctor than do younger folks and if their Doctor tells them something, many of them still take it as the Gospel and follow orders. I remember sitting in on a consultation with a physician and his patient who was a heavy smoker of tobacco, when I was the Nicotine Dependency Counselor. The Doctor pulled up his chair directly in front of this older man and said, "I've been your Doctor for a long time and you know that I have always had your best interest in mind. I have tried to keep you in the best health that I can. But I have to tell you now that you have Chronic Obstructive Pulmonary Disease and if you keep smoking cigarettes there is nothing that I can do to keep up with the damage that this is causing your lungs. You will be doomed to a gasping, lingering death. But you don't have to go there. You can quit and I have asked the Nicotine Dependency Counselor, Kal to help you get everything you need to do this. Will you accept the help?" That loving intervention by that Doctor made all the difference in the world and that man did accept help and got off tobacco.

One of the funniest interventions that I can recall from a middle-aged alcoholic in treatment was that his dog intervened on him. He said that he had a beagle named Buddy that he loved and who loved him. However, whenever he was drinking, Buddy would not come and sit with him and wanted nothing to do with him. Buddy would go and lie down under the coffee table and shun him. He said that this bothered him so much that he decided that he needed to go into treatment! I'm not saying that the "beagle intervention" would always work, but it does show the craving for love from somewhere that addicts have.

There can be other attempts made to try to talk an addict into treatment, but if these are one-on-one talks, they will rarely be effective. Addicts are such skillful manipulators that they will usually run circles around others that are trying to help them. One factor that dooms these individual chats to failure is the fact that the person trying to intervene believes that they have to speak logically to the addict, but the addict is not bound by logic. The addict can bring up anything from left field in an argument that has nothing to do with what is being talked about and run with that while the friend is left spinning. It is a little like being involved in a baseball game where one side believes that 3 strikes makes an out and 3 outs is the end of their half inning. They are playing by these rules, but the other side decides to not go by these rules. They suddenly say that they are getting 5 strikes per at-bat and 9 outs per inning! Who do you think is going to win that game? That is why people never win arguments with addicts. They don't play by the rules of logic. That is why one person alone is rarely successful. One voice crying in the wilderness of addiction is not enough usually to effect change for the addict.

Consequently, the process that will usually have the best chance for success is the planned intervention. The power of the group is something that addiction centers found out long ago. The preferred modality of treatment for addicted persons is group therapy, because the group has so much power. Addicts know that they can't bamboozle other addicts in a group and when they are trying to spout some self-serving "horse hockey" in group, they are going to be called on it every time by the group. As one group member put it to his dishonest fellow member, "You're not talking to the fans now – you're talking to the players"!

This same power of the group also works for a group of people who are trying to help an addict get into treatment in a planned intervention. When an addict is confronted with love by all the people who are important to her, it is the most powerful thing that can happen to motivate towards help. In fact, the vast majority of interventions lead to success.

If an intervention specialist is enlisted for the family intervention, the success rates are about 80 % on an average. I happen to know that my former colleague and good friend, Bruce Perkins, who is an intervention specialist, has a success rate of over 90% of addicts going to treatment immediately. If you count those who think things over for a while after the intervention and then go into treatment, the statistic is about 95%. That is remarkable. You may want to check out his website at www.bruceperkins.com. This costs some money, but when most families add up how much money they have already wasted on enabling behaviors that yielded nothing, they can see professional intervention as a bargain.

Family members and friends can gather together and assemble a team for a structured intervention without professional help, but it is a lot easier and goes better usually if an intervention specialist is used. Intervention specialists already know all of the things that family members will need to learn to do a successful intervention. The specialists know how to build a good team, which treatment centers would fit the needs of a particular addict, which centers take which kinds of health insurance, which centers are available if a person has no insurance and no money, the best place and time for an intervention and who should be included and excluded from the intervention. These are all things that are part of the daily work of an intervention specialist and they can do them almost automatically. There is a formula that has been proven to work in doing interventions and these professionals know what that formula is and use it well.

However, if a family does not have the money to hire a professional that does not mean that they can't do the intervention themselves. The easiest way for a family to do it yourself is to purchase the definitive book on interventions by Jeff Jay and Debra Jay entitled "Love First". This book is published by Hazelden, which is a national non-profit organization founded in 1949 that is dedicated to helping people deal with the addictive illness. Hazelden has an online bookstore at hazelden.org/bookstore and a phone number at 800-328-9000.

The book, "Love First" is very comprehensive and will walk a family through everything that they need to do to construct an effective intervention. As the title of the book implies, the key to getting an addict help is to let them know that they are loved in a way that they can finally hear it.

As we said before, addicts appear to be very insensitive by their behavior, but underneath that hard shell there is a soft, gooey part that has been longing for love and approval for a long time. Addicts end up pushing away the very thing that they crave, because they know that if they let other people in to see their true feelings it would make them vulnerable. They might then have to listen to their family members and friends and what these folks will be telling them is that they have to stop their addictive behavior. No addict wants to hear that message, so it is necessary to keep others at arm's length emotionally.

Addicts are people who have lost faith and have lost hope that anybody, including God, could ever love them. They can't love themselves because of guilt and shame and are sure that nobody else could love them either. Drugs have become their first love and they want to use them like the want to breathe. Anything that threatens that has to be knocked out of the sky before it touches them. They can't imagine life without drugs and they know they are not worthy of anybody's love because of it.

A structured intervention actually gives the addict what they have wanted all along and that is to be loved. There is something so powerful about a group of people who are gathered together to speak words of love and concern to an addict, that the addict can rarely resist their request to get help. When there is no judgment and no blame and no anger in the conversation the addict can listen. When there is honesty and specific concerns mixed with love, the addict can hear the message. The addict begins to believe that he or she is sick and not just bad.

When gathering a team for the intervention it is paramount to enlist as many people as possible whom the addict respects. These could be people that have influence over the addict such as: their physician, their boss and their minister. However, they could be just people that are highly respected such as: their grandfather, grandmother, co-worker or long-time friend. If some of these people cannot attend the planning sessions or the actual intervention, they can write a letter that will be read by the leader of the intervention.

Whoever is chosen as intervention leader must do some evaluation of the people who are invited to participate. Even if a certain person is influential, but has an active addiction problem themselves, they should not be invited. Anybody that the addict actually hates should be left out. Anybody that might reveal to the addict that an intervention is being planned should be left out. One of the sure ways to spoil a good intervention is to have the addict find out ahead of time so that they can steel themselves against the information and have their arguments all ready to refute that information. The element of surprise is important in this endeavor so that the addict does not have a chance to entrench themselves against the love and concern and information.

The treatment team should have between 4 and 10 members. Less than 4 doesn't feel like much of a group, but more than 10 is overkill and takes too long in the sharing section. Everybody on the team is asked to write down what they are going to say to the addict. All of these letters start out by saying that they love the addict and are concerned about them. They then go on to talk about the importance of the relationship and what the addict has meant to them in their life. The next part is to describe how the sickness has hurt the relationship, by giving very specific examples of this. It concludes by saying that they would like the addict to get help and be the person again that they know and love.

Before the time of the intervention all the details concerning treatment should be ironed out. A treatment center that is designed for the specific needs of an addict should always be considered. For example, medical detoxification should be available for chronic alcoholics, because alcoholic seizures without medical attention are fatal almost half the time. If a program is needed that does not require insurance or money up front, this should be researched. The distance away from home might make a difference in which center to choose. A treatment program that has an aftercare program is always good. A treatment program that uses the 12 steps of Alcoholics Anonymous and Narcotics Anonymous is preferred. Everything should be nailed down so that the addict can't give some excuse for not going. Job absenteeism should be taken care of, child care, transportation, insurance coverage and anything else that could be an excuse not to go to treatment has to be covered.

The next consideration is to choose the time and place of the intervention. The best time is sometime when the addict is not drunk or high. However, there are some addicted persons in a later stage of addiction that are pretty much high all the time. In these cases the team tries to pick a time when the addict is at least less intoxicated or not quite as high. Usually early in the morning is a better time to catch addicts than later in the day after they are loaded. The team may not find a perfect time, but must choose the best that they can.

The place of the intervention might be a little tricky too. Some addicts don't like to use when they are around their parents or grandparents, so waiting for a weekend when they will be at their family's home might be the ideal time to intervene. Going over to a best friend's home for dinner might be another good place for the intervention. Sometimes an addict is looking to score a little money from grandma and he will come over any time grandma calls and invites him over. Grandma's house could be the ideal spot for the intervention.

When the addict arrives at the designated place, the leader greets them and asks them to be seated in a spot further from the door. He announces that there are many people here who love the addict and want to share some personal things with him or her. Each member of the team reads their brief letter of love and concern. The team does not get into discussion with the addict, because this will derail the process. Usually the most influential person reads their letter last. When everybody has finished reading their letters, the leader asks if the addict will accept help and get well. If the addict says that they will get help, they are told that everything has been arranged and all they have to do is get in the car or on the plane and start the process. If there are objections, the team leader answers these quickly and then the bags are already packed and they go.

There are a small percentage of addicts who will refuse the help offered and they may even start to storm out of the room. At this point the team leader suggests that it would be in their best interests to listen to what the team has decided to do. These things are called either "the consequences", "the bottom line" or "the resolutions". These are things that team members have decided ahead of time that they will do differently if the addict chooses not to take the help offered. These things are not punishments, they are simply things the team will no longer do to support the disease. They make it clear that they are always there to support the person, but not their disease. The same loving tone is used to share these consequences as was used in the letter.

Examples of consequences might be things like: "You can no longer live here if you don't get help", "we will not pay for your college if you don't get treatment, "I am moving out if you don't get help", "I will call the police the next time I know you are out driving drunk" and "I won't cover for you at work anymore when you are hung over". There are many other things that might be considered as appropriate leverage to pry somebody into treatment that really needs to go, but refuses.

Even if the person refuses to go to treatment, the intervention has been successful. It is a success because the family members and friends have finally dealt with the real issue and can now get some help for themselves and their codependency. In addition the family is no longer tiptoeing around the elephant in the living room pretending it is not there. But it is also successful, because it will be harder to keep the addiction going without all the well-meaning, but misguided helpers making it easier to keep using. Oftentimes addicts that refuse treatment right away will come around after a while and decide that they will get help anyway. Thus, all interventions are successful at some level.

After treatment the team is prepared to support ongoing recovery, which should include aftercare counseling, attendance at 12-Step meetings and getting a sponsor.

To sum up, if we love an addicted person, we don't have to wait until they hit bottom – we can help bring bottom up to hit them. That way they can recover before the disease is so advanced that it kills them. There are several ways to intervene and if they are done with love, they all help.

16

Cross Dependency

One of the greatest obstacles to recovery for addicted persons is the phenomenon called "cross dependency". This is also sometimes called "switched addiction". What these phrases mean is that it looks like switching from one addictive agent to another is a softer, easier way than quitting all addictive substances altogether. It reminds me of an old cigarette advertisement for Tareyton cigarettes that showed the picture of a man with a black eye smoking a Tareyton. The caption said, "He would rather fight than switch". With addicted persons it is exactly the opposite. They would rather switch than fight. They would rather take the pressure off from their families or other concerned persons by switching addictive agents to something that sounds less harmful or dangerous.

For example, a cocaine addict might tell his family that he had quit using coke, but he has started using amphetamines instead. A heroin user might tell her husband that she has stopped shooting up heroin and is just using some Vicodin now and again. There are countless persons that I have worked with over the years who were acting very proud of the fact that they have stopped illegal drugs and proclaimed that they "just drink alcohol now". When I worked with nicotine dependency, tobacco addicts would believe that they were in recovery from smoking, because they were just chewing tobacco. The current rage for nicotine addicts is to be all excited about quitting cigarettes, but they are "vaping" instead. Other addicts that I talk to tell me that they are "off the sauce", because of DUI's and are just smoking a little weed now. They usually say it as if I should be impressed, but I'm not impressed.

What cross dependency means is that there is a cross over in the brain for anyone who is addicted on one substance to any other substance that can make a person feel "high". The human brain doesn't really make much of a distinction between one addictive agent and the next. All the brain knows is either high or not high. If a person can get high on one addictive substance, they can get high on another.

What addicts don't understand and don't really want to understand is that if they are addicted to one thing, they are addicted to anything that is mood-altering and that includes substances that they have never even tried before. I was making this point in group therapy the other day and I asked a young female addict to tell me a drug that she had never used before. She said she had never tried heroin. I said to her, "Well, you are addicted to heroin". "How could I be", she shouted, "I just told you I had never used it"! "No", I replied, "but heroin can get you high too and you are addicted to the high".

An example that I have used before in group therapy to try to help patients understand cross dependency is to compare it to horseback riding. "Have you ever been horseback riding", I ask them?" Some usually have tried it. "Have you ever gotten saddle sores on the top of your rear end from where the saddle rubs on you", I inquire? Some have experienced this. "Imagine that you come back from riding with your saddle sores and tell yourself that you have got to get off this big black horse because it is killing your hind end. So, you jump off the black horse and turn around and get on a big white horse and ride away. You only get a half mile down the lane when you realize that the white horse is killing your posterior also. You go back, get off and tie up the white horse and then decide you need to do something very different. You jump on a jackass and ride away. What do you think will happen?" The patients usually get it by this point and say, "I would have more saddle sores". "That's right", I respond. "So what is the problem here? Is it that you just haven't found the right kind of horse or is the problem riding, period"? "The problem is riding", they answer.

This is the issue when it comes to cross dependency. Riding is riding is riding and using is using is using. It doesn't matter which horse you are riding just as it doesn't matter which addictive substance you are using. The problem is that you are still using. An addicted person is addicted to anything that can change their mood in a hurry. It doesn't have to be the addict's favorite agent. Anything that changes the mood in a hurry will do in a pinch.

One area of delusional thinking for addicted persons is that they believe that if they switch from something that is illegal to something that is legal, it is fine for them to keep using this new, legal substance. Folks who have either burned out or gotten in legal trouble with illegal substances like cocaine, heroin, methamphetamines and marijuana will oftentimes just give up trying to fight the system and switch to getting drunk. They are usually very proud of this change and say things like, "I used to use hard drugs, but I was able to quit on my own and don't do that anymore." When an addict leads with that kind of statement I am always prepared to follow up by asking them if they are not using "hard drugs", what are the "soft drugs" that they are using? The answer is usually that they are "just drinking" or "just smoking pot". They tend to get rather indignant when I am not properly impressed with this switch.

I am regularly surprised at how vehemently addicts argue in favor of the use of marijuana. If you want to have a fight on your hands in group therapy on Psychiatry, just challenge the patient's statements about the benefits and justifications for using marijuana. You will hear things like the following. "Weed should be legal and in some states it is legal, so I should be able to use that". "Marijuana is a natural plant, so it is not harmful to you". "I don't ever get violent or crazy when I smoke weed like I do when I do cocaine". "Marijuana really helps me with my pain and I have to have it." "I can't give up everything and pot seems to keep me calm and I don't get into trouble with pot".

When I point out that marijuana is not legal in this state yet and could potentially cause legal problems, the response is almost always, "Well, it should be legal". I point out that just because something is a natural plant, that doesn't mean it is not harmful. For example, I have some Nightshade weeds growing in my pasture and if you touch it, it will give you a horrible rash worse than poison ivy. If cattle eat it, it kills them. It is a natural plant, but it can be deadly. Actually, a lot of drugs come from natural plants like coca leaves and poppy seed, etc. but that doesn't mean they aren't dangerous. What about corn? We have a lot of corn in Indiana and that is a natural plant, but they can make corn liquor out of it! But of course, the biggest objection to switching to marijuana is that the person is still getting high. How can a person learn how to handle their feelings in a natural way when something unnatural is taking care of their feelings for them?

But by far, the biggest current delusion of cross dependency is the notion that if a person gets drugs prescribed from their Doctor, then they can't be harmful. I keep hearing this phrase over and over again by people that are dependent on prescription drugs. "But I got these pills from my Doctor"! That may be true and that Doctor may have had the best intentions, but it doesn't make a bit of difference to the brain of the person using those drugs. The human brain can't tell the difference between something you purchased from a shady character illegally in a back alley and something that you picked up in a nice, clean pharmacy that was prescribed by a nice, clean, helpful Doctor. All the brain knows is loaded or not loaded, anesthetized or not anesthetized.

As we discussed earlier in the chapter on painful feelings, the medical profession is under intense pressure to make sure that their patients in and out of the hospital do not experience pain. Thus, we have the situation that exists today with physicians prescribing more and more addictive drugs and patients demanding better and better pain control. Older patients in particular tend to be much more compliant with what their physician says they should do and if they are prescribed something for nervousness or for pain that is habit forming, they tend to take it with no questions asked.

I was reading some statistics recently about dependency in older Americans. It said that it is estimated that as many as 80% of senior citizens are taking one or more mood-altering substances. Certainly, as people get older they have more aches and pains, but that hardly justifies the rampant prescribing of synthetic narcotics to seniors. There are also a startling number of seniors taking anti-anxiety medications like the Benzodiazepenes. This would include medications like: Librium, Valium, Xanax and Ativan. One would not think that seniors would have that many things to get anxious about, but they are using a lot of these types of medications just the same.

There is a strong tendency to switch back and forth between these anti-anxiety medications and ethyl alcohol, because chemically they are about the same thing. When I worked on an inpatient drug/alcohol treatment center, our physicians used to regularly prescribe Librium as a medication to safely, medically detoxify alcoholics. This is a good practice, because without being stepped down gradually from alcohol with something like Librium, alcoholics can go into alcoholic seizures, which is very dangerous. Without proper medical attention, if an alcoholic goes into alcoholic seizing, they stand a 50% chance of dying. People don't generally realize that from just a physical withdrawal standpoint, alcohol withdrawal is by far the most dangerous drug there is. It is far more dangerous than heroin, cocaine or anything else in terms of just physical withdrawal.

So, it is certainly good practice to use a Benzodiazepene medicine for detoxification, because it really is pretty much freeze dried booze or booze in a pill as we used to say on the detoxification unit. These medicines can be used to step down a person gradually off booze and keep them safe from seizures and possible death. However, this is not something that should be substituted for alcohol on a long-term basis, because drinking and taking these pills means basically the same thing.

Part of the disease of addiction is to be always looking for a "softer, easier way" as the A.A. Big Book puts it. This is how folks get into addictions, by seeking that quick fix and easier way out of their problems and uncomfortable feelings. But that is not how people get out of an addiction. Cross dependency is a sick part of seeking that softer, easier way. It is still displaying the same attitude of looking for something outside to be brought in to take care of inside things in the individual. The only difference is not a change of the person, but just a change of the substance. As we said before, riding is still riding and using is still using.

Something that is currently in fashion in the world of addiction treatment is the substitution of medicines like Methadone, Suboxone and Subutex instead of using narcotics. These medicines are supposed to be regulated better and can be stepped down so that the narcotics addict will no longer have to use them. They will also prevent withdrawal symptoms from narcotics, which are certainly horrible. But the problem that I see at least in our area of the country is that none of the addicts ever seem to get off these medications. They don't seem to be stepped down. I run into addicts all the time that have been on Methadone for years. They tell me that the physical withdrawal symptoms from Methadone are actually much worse than withdrawing from heroin, so they never want to do that. To my way of thinking, that is nothing more than switching one drug for another. The only thing that seems helpful about it is that at least you don't have narcotics addicts robbing convenience stores to get their drugs. They can just go to a nice, clean clinic and get their drugs handed to them regularly for free. It may save on crimes committed to get drugs or money for drugs, but all in all I don't see much recovery in this program.

Most addiction specialists who work with this disease all the time will tell you that if we could get addicts to understand cross dependency or switched addiction as it is also called, we could prevent a huge percentage of the relapses that happen after an addict has been clean and sober for a time. Cross dependency is a major part of the delusion that an addict has that she is doing something about her addiction when she really is not. It is similar to someone making the crazy statement that they would never shoot themselves in the head with a pistol, but they would be alright doing that with a rifle! Or maybe they would be really different and say that they wouldn't shoot themselves, but would just stick a knife in their heart. That's different, but it's not real different. The result is always the same in cross dependency, only the addictive agent changes.

17

The Role of Religion in Recovery

As we stated in the chapter on addiction as a spiritual disease, "spirituality" and "religion" are not the same thing. Every human is spiritual, but not every person is religious. However, there are a lot of folks not only in our culture, but every culture that have some religious background. No matter what religious group one is affiliated with there are some things in common. Religions attempt to define, delineate and understand that which is beyond our existence.

Whether a person attends worship in a mosque, a synagogue, a church or worships nature in the outdoors, there is within each one of us a desire to not only know about some kind of Higher Power, but to be in the good graces of that Power. We want to know not only who our God is, but more importantly, what does that God think of people and more to the point, what does He think of me? Am I alright with God in the eternal scheme of things? There appears to be a sense of accountability to God that human beings have. We seem to need to justify our existence in some way so that we can let God know that there is a reason why He should continue to accept us, love us and let us live a little longer.

On my good days, I believe that there are so many different religions and so many different denominations within religions, because each group wants to make the best use of God or their Higher Power that they can. They each believe that their particular understanding of that Higher Power helps people to be close to and utilize that Power in the best way. The Christians believe they added the right understandings of God that Judaism didn't have. The Muslims believe they improved upon the Christian understanding of God and so on. Within Christianity, the Lutherans believed they needed to reform the Roman church and the other Protestant groups believed that the Lutherans didn't go far enough in reforming to have the best picture of who God is and what He wants.

That is what I think on my good days; my more positive days. On my bad days and more cynical days, I believe that there is so much division and so many different religions and denominations purely because of ecclesiastical one-ups-man-ship. In other words it looks like religious false pride that says, "We have the corner on the market of the true word of God and you don't". That is another way of saying, "we're right and you're wrong". People love being right.

On my regular days I believe that the proliferation of religious groups is probably a combination of the positive and the not so positive motivations. There is some genuine concern for truth and some need to be more right than the others.

Whatever the motivation might be and whatever religious group we might examine, there are some common themes in religion that continually show up that turn out to be either helpful or damaging to recovery from addictions. In some ways religion is kind of like high stakes poker for addicted persons. They can win a lot. But they can also lose a lot. There are extremists in all religions.

One of the most prevalent ways that addicts can lose by having religion is if they have been affiliated with a religious group that views addiction as a sin instead of as a disease. I have some familiarity with world religions, but I am better qualified to talk about Christianity, because it is the religion that I claim and that I know, so I'll stick with that.

Within Christianity there are some denominations, some individual congregations and some pastors who are on the right track in understanding addiction as a disease and they treat it like any other disease. However, there are too many folks in the church who do not do this. They come down very strongly that addiction is a sin and needs repentance. People who are addicted are thus seen as "bad" and not "sick". They are bad sinners in need of repentance instead of sick people in need of healing. There seems to be a fear in these groups that calling addiction a disease somehow leaves them off the moral hook and they don't want anybody left off the hook. They view other Christians who do not have this judgmental attitude as being "weak" and "wishy-washy". They believe you have to call a spade a spade and call a sin a sin.

This is the kind of attitude that will keep addicts drinking and using for a long time, because they are already filled with guilt and shame. They already are feeling terrible about themselves because they make resolutions to quit using and then break them sometimes on the same day. They already feel the weight of their sick behaviors caused by their disease. Some of the symptoms of addiction that we talked about before are a lowering of moral standards and a loss of values. When addicts do sick things that are against their morals and values like: ignore their families, fly into rages, spend all the household money on drugs and lie about almost everything to cover up, they feel guilty to start with. Then when some self-righteous preacher or church member lays a little more guilt on them by telling them that their using is a sin, it just drives them underground further and separates them from God even more.

For those Christians who are worried about going soft on sin it might be helpful to remember that we believe that all diseases are ultimately a result of sin. We live in a fallen, broken world that includes war, pain, heartache, disease and death and that is all the result of sin and disobedience to God. But to single out one disease, addiction, and make that the poster child of sin is neither fair nor helpful. All the other diseases like cancer, heart disease and strokes are also part of living in a sinful world, but we don't single people out with these diseases and call them "sinners". Of course they are sinners, as we all are, but not just because they have cancer or any other disease and we shouldn't do it with the disease of addiction.

I have talked to many pastors over the years that have trouble either understanding or accepting addiction as a disease. When I asked one of them what he did with the addicts in his congregation he told me that they didn't have any addicts in his congregation. I found that to be very interesting. Since practically every family has some addiction problems somewhere in the extended family it would be hard for me to imagine a large congregation that had nobody with any addiction problem. That sounds like clergy fantasy talk.

However, I did believe him that he didn't counsel with any addicts, because once folks found out about his moralistic stance concerning addictions, they wouldn't be talking to him about it, that's for sure. I suspect that addicts would go underground with their addiction issues and then not come back to church. They may have been looking for something in religion to help their vague spiritual desires, but they weren't going to find it there and unfortunately, it usually would sour them on going to any other religious gatherings that might have helped.

Another obstacle to recovery that some religious folks have erected is to insist that any talk about a nebulous "Higher Power" be done away with. A rule of thumb that I have discovered is that the more fundamentalist a church group is, the more trouble they tend to have with understanding and accepting the 12-Step way of recovery. They rebel at addicts in recovery speaking about their "Higher Power" and insist that this is not "God-specific" enough. They insist that addicts must speak of God at the very least and preferably speak about Jesus Christ as their Savior and do away with this vague "Higher Power" stuff.

This shows a great lack of understanding of where most addicts are starting from spiritually speaking. Most addicts have been running from God for some time because of the guilt and shame that drives addiction. Many have no religious background at all in understanding a very specific Christian notion of God. They are the fortunate ones. The others have what we have just been talking about in the previous section, namely, a very harsh, judgmental religious view of God. As I stated before, I would rather work with an addict that has no religious background at all than one with a slew of judgmental, fear-based, guilt-ridden notions of God.

There is no point in laying a bunch of theological fine points on a newly recovering addict. They are not at a place to take this in and utilize it. They are at a place where they are wondering if there might be some kind of God out there somewhere and if He could accept them. They are not ready for theological discussions of the predestination controversy or distinguishing the two natures of Christ or any theological jargon like that. St. Paul urged folks to give new Christians the "milk of the Word". What that means is that you don't throw beef steaks to babies. They have to start with mother's milk and move on up to something a little more complex in the food chain later on.

The same thing is true for addicts. They have to start where they can start, not where others would like them to start. They have to first come to the realization that there could actually be a Higher Power somewhere and that that Power is on their side to help them. As one of my recovering friends put it, "I had to realize that there was a God and that it was not me"! The next step for him was to surrender to that Higher Power and believe it was there trying to help him.

Many times the thought of a Supreme Being is too lofty for an addict and they must start simply believing that their 12-Step group together has more power to help them than they had by themselves. It is the difference between taking 12 pencils and breaking them one at a time and putting all 12 together and trying to break them all at once. They come to see that the group and the program and the readings all give them more power to stay sober and clean for one day than they had by themselves. As recovery goes on there becomes a deeper understanding of that "something" that is out there and usually recovering people find their way to a more God-specific understanding of that Higher Power. Then they may be ready to begin some more religious things to enhance their relationship with their God as they are starting to understand Him.

Another way that religion is not helpful in recovery is when a group or a pastor is very well-meaning and very accepting of the addict. One would not think that this could be a problem, because it is the opposite of the judgmental, moralistic, sin-admonishing attitude we looked at earlier. But the problem comes in when the pastor, in particular, offers forgiveness too quickly. Yes, forgiveness should always be part of the equation, but only when done at the right time.

As we saw earlier, addicts need pain in order to be properly motivated to change. Sometimes an addict will go to counsel with a pastor who is an understanding, loving and gracious person and will spill to him what has been going on with their addictive behavior. That pastor will then pronounce absolution on them and tell them that God loves them and they are alright now. This sound nice, but all it does is patch up the addict so that they can go out and use a little longer. It is putting a band-aid on something that requires surgery first. This well-meaning clergy person has short-circuited the pain that is necessary for surrender. Without surrender of the will to a Higher Power there is no recovery. There is definitely a place for absolution, but not before the surrender. It is the right impulse, but at the wrong time.

On an average, clergy delay treatment for addicts by about 4 years. It can be from being judgmental or from the opposite, granting forgiveness too soon. If religious folks need a Scriptural reference on this, just point them to the Old Testament prophets. The Lord always forgave the children of Israel for chasing after other gods and for neglecting the disadvantaged in their midst. However, there always had to be pain to make the Israelites turn back to God. They usually had to suffer the consequences of being run over by one world power or another before they came to their senses. First there was their surrender and then the forgiveness and closeness. It is like that in addiction recovery also. Taking away the pain too soon is just as harmful as never taking it away.

Actually, in most cases pastors and other religious leaders won't be talking to addicted persons nearly as much as they will the family members of these addicts. Addicts tend to keep a distance from church many times because guilt always causes separation. However, many times spouses or children or parents of addicts will come and speak to a pastor about their concerns over a loved one's using. Hopefully, that pastor will be prepared to be helpful.

Pastors will oftentimes be dealing with codependents and not know it. Pastors really like codependents in their congregation whether they know that is the case or not, because these people do a lot of work in the church. I have known many women in particular, who have very little going on at home in terms of a close relationship, because their husband has a closer relationship with alcohol and drugs. These women get their self-worth from serving in the church. They are there whenever the doors are open, cleaning things, setting things up and attending things. They don't get their needs met at home, but do get them met by being involved in church. Some pastors actually encourage this by praising this behavior, but this is rather self-serving. They would do better to help these codependents get their relationship back at home by helping the family to gain chemical health.

We have talked about many of the negatives that "bad religion" can have on recovery. But make no mistake; there are many huge benefits that healthy religion can give to recovering families. The spiritual growth and understanding of a person's Higher Power can help immensely in recovery. Building spiritual habits such as: worship, prayer, meditation and uplifting readings sets a foundation for further spiritual growth.

In healthy congregations people share with one another their spiritual struggles. This gives the addicted family the permission to talk about their own struggles. This is essential in dealing with both guilt and shame. As we said before, guilt needs confession and absolution and shame needs exposure to heal. The Christian church can be a safe haven for doing both of these things. There is nothing like rubbing elbows with a few sinners every Sunday to help one feel accepted by them and by God. Further education in understanding God's attitude towards people is available. Opportunities to serve are always present. It is important for an addicted person to learn how to give instead of take, because users don't just use drugs – they use people. Learning how good it feels to give with no expectation of reward is a very gratifying thing. Experiencing the mystical connection to the Lord in the body and blood of Christ in Holy Communion cannot be explained, but it can be felt. We also have grape juice available at Communion for recovering addicts, by the way at my congregation. All of these great things can be available to addicts in a healthy church.

There are certain things that a clergy person can do to be better prepared to deal with addictions properly. If I were a pastor going to a new congregation in a different area I would do the following things. I would get a list of where the 12-Step meetings are in that area and ask around as to which might be the healthiest meetings for dependents and codependents. I would search and find a man and a woman that are in solid recovery and are working a good recovery program. These are people that I could call at any hour of the day or night and ask them to talk to an addict that needs help. They would be willing to do this, because helping others helps them to stay clean and sober too. I would find out what treatment centers are in the area and what kind of patients they would admit. For instance, if they don't have medical detoxification I might refer somewhere else. If they don't accept patients who have no insurance and no money, I might have to go elsewhere. Another thing I would do is find out where the nearest intervention specialist is located and put him or her on speed-dial.

Pastors can't know everything and they can't do everything. It is important for them to know the people who are expert in things that they are not and refer to them. I have discovered an inversely proportional ratio in pastors. Those with the most education and experience tend to refer to other experts the most. Those with the least education and experience try to handle all situations in the parish themselves. The latter is not a good idea.

Churches and pastors who are open and accepting can help recovery a great deal before and after treatment. Addicts have been seeking love for a long time while desperately using and will unfold like a flower when they get that love and acceptance at the right time. If a congregation looks like a hospital for sinners instead of a museum where the saints go get dusted off once a week, it will attract recovering people and it will help them. The atmosphere of a congregation and a pastor should say, "This is a place for folks who tend to screw up from time to time and God still loves them and so do we".

18

Relapse

We have talked a lot about the difficulties addicts have in recognizing that they need help and the struggles that family members and friends have in assisting addicts in getting help. However, it is important to remember that even after treatment there is a good chance that the addicted person will relapse and start using their addictive agent again. This might be for any number of reasons, which we will examine more closely.

Those who care about an addicted person are often devastated when they go through all the pain, the time, the expense and the drama of intervening on an addict and finally manage to get them into treatment, only to see them get out of treatment and relapse. There is the sinking feeling that treatment may work for some people, but apparently not for our loved one and that everything that was done is a huge waste of time and energy.

That is not true, however. No intervention is ever a waste of time, because if the addict chooses not to get well, the family still benefits with their own recovery from codependency. But even more than that, every intervention is valuable also to the addicted person, because at least the door of mental health has been opened for them and they know what can be done if they so choose. If they choose not to walk through that door, they at least had and still have a chance to do so.

It is comforting to family members to realize that relapse is very much a part of the disease of addiction. Relapse doesn't mean that recovery can't happen; it just means that the addict probably needs a little more pain before they are willing to do whatever it takes to stay well. There is a saying in Alcoholics Anonymous circles that describes this need for further pain in order to get serious about recovery. That phrase is, "I guess he just needed to do a little more research"!

As we said before, recovery is not an event; it is a process. As my dairy farmer friend put it, "Recovery is a lot less like going to the circus to see the elephant and a lot more like milking the same cows every day". There are certain tasks that need to be done every day in order for recovery to continue. Without the daily work that recovery takes there will very soon be no recovery.

Another way of saying this is that relapse is the default position of recovery. It is not like there are some addicts that might relapse. They will all relapse unless there is the ongoing work every day that it takes to not relapse.

I have shared with patients in treatment a visualization of what recovery and relapse look like. I ask them to imagine that they are in a large department store that has escalators that carry people up and down. Sometimes when we were kids we used to run up the down escalator just for fun. We had to take the steps up the escalator just a little bit faster than that escalator was pulling us down. That is basically what recovery is like. An addicted person has to take the steps (and there are 12 or them) a little faster than the downward pull of their disease.

If you are standing on that escalator, you don't have to run down the steps to fall on your face at the bottom. All you have to do is nothing! If you simply stand still for a long enough time, the disease will pull you down to crash and burn all on its own. So relapse is oftentimes not the result of making a calculated decision to drink or use again, it is simply the absence of doing the right things that would prevent a return to using. It is then not a case of deciding to do bad things, but rather a reluctance to do enough good things.

There are predictable signs that relapse is already occurring. If an addict gets out of treatment, but does not continue with her outpatient aftercare meetings, this almost always signifies that she believes she is "cured" or "recovered" instead of recovering. The following paragraphs describe how relapse happens.

Non-attendance of 12-Step meetings is a sure sign of this same kind of "cured" thinking. 12-Step recovery groups are by far the most successful fellowships for helping addicts and their families stay in recovery. The 12-Step program has been tried and true for many decades in helping folks get well. Nobody runs 12-Step groups, so there is no axe to grind. They are pure fellowships that only exist to "share their experience, strength and hope". There are religiously sponsored recovery groups too and they have helped people be in recovery, but it has always struck me as sort of reinventing the wheel when the 12-Step groups are already proven and available and are spiritual in nature. But all recovery groups help.

If a person has been attending meetings and relapses, one of the first things to look at is if they went to enough meetings. One meeting per week is not much to combat a fatal disease. Many treatment centers recommend 90 meetings in 90 days after treatment to make sure that the addict is immersed in recovery right away. I have several recovering friends that attend more meetings now than they did 25 or 30 years ago when they first began recovery. They are not going to the meetings now as they did at first just to try to hang on by their fingernails and be sober one more day. They are attending the meetings to learn better how to live spiritually, the first part of which is being sober for a day.

Getting a sponsor will prevent relapse. A person coming out of treatment or beginning recovery in the fellowship of 12-Step groups should ask to have a temporary sponsor at their very first meeting. That way they can have someone to call at any hour of the day or night when they struggle with negative, using thoughts. After they have attended a number of meetings they can then ask someone to be their permanent sponsor. The qualifications for a good sponsor should be someone of your own gender, someone who has been continuously clean and sober for at least two years, someone who attends meetings regularly and someone that makes sense when they talk.

Another sign of relapse is if a recovering person does not call their sponsor regularly. An addict doesn't have to worry about being a nuisance to their sponsor by too many calls, because that sponsor wants to stay straight too and the struggles of addicts newly sponsored helps them to relive that from their own recovery and renews their resolve to continue their own recovery. I encourage recovering persons to call their sponsor every day, because they will be in the habit of doing it and on those tough days when they really should be talking to somebody, they will be talking to somebody, because they do it every day.

If a recovering person believes that he or she can still associate with their old using buddies, they are already relapsing. We had a young man in treatment one time that told his group that he was still going to go to his favorite bar with his old using buddies, but he was just going to drink soda pop. One of the older members of the group who had some relapse experience began laughing at him. The young man was offended and asked, "What are you laughing at"? The old-timer replied succinctly, "Well, you don't go to a whorehouse just to get kissed and alcoholics don't go to bars to drink soda pop"! That pretty much said it all.

Loneliness and isolating can be a recipe for relapse as well. One of the tough things about recovery is that an addict has no idea what to do all alone and no buddies to do anything with. An addict usually expects that he will have all kinds of tempting offers from his former using buddies to go use with them and he is prepared to withstand the onslaught. In reality it is more likely that his old using buddies will leave him alone for a while to test his wind and then nobody calls and it is lonely. Isolating allows self-pity to creep in and as they say in A.A. "Self-pity is poor me, poor me, pour me another drink"!

A similar problem to loneliness is simply having too much free time. If an addict doesn't have healthy activities to occupy her time, she will always start thinking of unhealthy things to do. So, if a person is unemployed or disabled and cannot work, they need to find some ways to volunteer. There are hundreds of causes that need volunteers and doing something constructive will not only occupy time, but give a sense of purpose and a way to give back to the community.

Something that is oftentimes overlooked as a relapse danger is when an addict also has a mental illness as well as addiction. This is known as having a "co-morbid illness". If a person has Bipolar Disorder or Clinical Depression, they will need medications to bring their mood to a more normal level. If they have Schizophrenia they will need an anti-psychotic medication. They obviously need to quit drinking or using other drugs first, however. Addiction is a primary disease. There is no way for example, that a person with depression can keep using a central nervous system depressant drug like alcohol and stay out of depression. That is like saying you want to put out a fire, but grab a can of gasoline and throw it on the fire. The other thing that most psychiatric patients don't understand is that their psychiatric medications will not work if they keep using alcohol or other drugs. Those chemicals render the psychiatric medications ineffective. They may have started using drugs and alcohol as a way to self-medicate their psychiatric illness, but it is a poor medication and will keep the real medication from doing its work.

One sure-fire way to swirl back down the toilet of addiction is for an addict to hang onto resentments and anger. The Big Book of

Alcoholics Anonymous makes it plain that "Resentment is the number one offender. It kills more alcoholics than anything else..." It goes on to describe how holding onto anger and letting it ferment inside a person shuts off the sunlight of the spirit and the person will return to drinking or using. Resentments are simply anger issues that a person has been sitting on for a long time. Resentments are further described as being "fatal". An addict must let these things go or it kills them.

If a recovering person keeps relapsing even though they are going to meetings and have a sponsor and are doing other good recovery things, it is almost always because of unresolved shame issues. As we stated before, shame is that feeling of worthlessness that comes to us because somebody else has treated us as if we are worthless, dirty and bad. Physical abuse and verbal abuse are common in the backgrounds of addicts, but particularly addicts who keep relapsing. But the shame that seems to run deeper and destroy more self-worth comes from sexual abuse. There is something so insidious and personal about sexual abuse that if left covered up, it will keep poisoning any good changes that an addict might start to make. Just when they start to feel better about themselves, they remember that they really are bad and worthless and don't deserve anything good in life and then they pull the whole structure of recovery down around their ears and relapse.

As we said, some relapse comes from making poor decisions to do dangerous things in slippery places with unhealthy people and then relapse occurs. However, there are more relapses that happen simply because there is not enough maintenance doing healthy things. It is a little like having an automobile and enjoying the way that it takes you from point A to Point B. However, you never change the oil, never check any of the belts and don't pay any attention to those little warning lights on your dash. You shouldn't be surprised when it stops working. It had no maintenance.

A story I shared with our Aftercare Group was the story of "The

Low Maintenance Horse". Once upon a time there was an old man who loved horses. He was getting on in years and was a bit senile, but he still liked to work with horses and thought everyone should have a horse. He felt it would keep people more sane and grounded. He was telling his old buddy that he decided that what folks needed was a good low maintenance horse, because they were rather expensive to own. He said he found an intelligent-looking sorrel gelding and was working with him to train him to be low maintenance. He cut him down to three-quarters ration of oats and hay and he was doing great. He cut him down to half rations and he still was doing fine. He cut him down to where he wasn't eating hardly anything at all, but then he said to his friend that unfortunately, the horse up and died on him and he would have to start over with another horse!

This is in effect, what a lot of recovering people try to do. They want to be the low maintenance horse and just cut back on their spiritual nourishment until they aren't taking in hardly any at all and then wonder why they relapse.

So, relapse is part of the disease of addiction and will happen without the proper maintenance. If relapse does happen it will be necessary to remind the addict of the relapse agreement that they signed in treatment and remind them of the bottom line consequences if they do not get back in recovery. They will hopefully try it again and be successful.

19

Having a Program

Because relapse is the default position of recovery as we said in the last chapter, it is essential that the addicted person have an ongoing program of recovery to offset the constant downward pull of the disease.

Many times when I have asked a person who is either afflicted or affected by the addictive illness what their plan of recovery is, they don't seem to know. They say things like, "Well, I'm just going to not drink or use anymore". Codependents will say, I'm just not going to let it bother me anymore". That sounds nice, but it really means nothing. When I ask them how they are going to do this, they really don't have a clue. They are just hoping that having a desire to be different will make it so. They don't have a plan; all they have is a goal. Yes, the goal is to get well and be clean and sober, but what are the steps that will make that happen? The goal for codependents is to emotionally detach without abandoning, but how are they going to get to that place?

This is why recovering people must have a program of recovery. Recovery is not an event; it is a process. That process takes some measureable and observable actions in order to reach the goal. For example, when soldiers are going into battle against an enemy, they don't just say, "Well we've got men and guns and they have men and guns. Let's just fire away and see what happens"! No, there is always a battle plan which takes into account what resources are available, how these resources could be used and when they should be used. Successful attacks have a plan and everybody knows what the plan is and does their part of that plan.

In the same way, recovery has to be viewed as a war against an enemy that is trying to kill you and that enemy is the disease of addiction. You have to have a battle plan and carry out that plan. You also have to go at it with everything you have. Nobody ever won a battle going into it at half speed. An addict will either go at recovery like they mean it or it won't happen. It is literally do or die, because addiction is a fatal disease. It is not like addiction might kill you - it is killing you and only the plan of recovery will save from death.

Having a program for this disease is not really all that different from having a program for any other disease. For example, several years ago I had my annual health screening at the hospital and I asked for the option of having a health coach that would call me once a month to check up on me and make sure I was doing what I needed to do. I'll never forget our first conversation. Her name was Beth and she said, "I have the results of your tests and here's the deal. You can keep eating two helpings at every meal with three starches per meal like you are now and you can sit on your duff and not exercise like you are now and you will be a diabetic in a very short time. Or, you could push away from the table, cut down on starches, begin walking at least 2 miles per day and do some exercises and not be a diabetic. Which do you want"? At that point I choked a little and said, "I think I want that not-a-diabetic thing". "Well then here's the plan", Beth said to me.

There was certainly a part of me that said "I don't like this". But then I remember what my old supervisor used to tell me. He would always say, "Yeah, Kal, you don't have to like it. Liking it is optional.

You just have to do it". So I began doing it. The plan was very specific with measureable and observable actions so that I would know and Beth would know if I was actually accomplishing my goal of health by what I was doing in my plan.

Part of my plan was some built-in accountability. I knew that if I didn't have Beth checking in on me every month, reviewing my actions for physical, mental and spiritual health, I would tend to slide back into the way I usually do things. In a similar way for a recovery plan for addicts, there always has to be some accountability. That is why it is so important for a recovering addict to have a sponsor. To be accountable to another is very motivating. It is the very reason why true fellowships like Alcoholics Anonymous, Narcotics Anonymous and Alanon have the greatest success with the most people; there is accountability built into the fellowships.

Another aspect of the recovering fellowships that is effective is that the individual with the illness no longer feels as if they are alone. They have felt that they must be the weirdest, most degenerate, most disgusting person on earth and then they find that they are not alone. They find that they are just like everybody else who has their disease and in a way, discover that they are "normal" according to the others who have the same disease. As one recovering man told me about his experience in the fellowship of Narcotics Anonymous, "I decided that I needed to get honest with my group and I just started sharing some of the nasty things I had done. After every example I shared almost every one of the group members said, "Yep, I've done that. I know how you feel".

The feeling of being in the same boat with others is why most programs of change work better than going it alone. The most successful exercise programs that I have ever had, for example, are ones that I did with a group of other people. On those days when I didn't feel like exercising, one of the others would pump me up and get me to exercise anyway. Then on days when he didn't feel like exercising, I would jab him into doing it anyway. It is a form of Higher Power that is more than just me by myself to motivate me to do what I need to do, but don't necessarily want to do.

Again, the more specific a plan is, the easier it is for a person to know if they are following that plan or not. So, one part of a recovery plan should be to attend 12-Step meetings, but that is not enough. The specifics should include how many meetings per week are going to be attended, which meetings these are going to be and what painful issues are going to be shared at each of these meetings. The plan should include having a sponsor, but that needs to be nailed down as well. It should sound something like "I will ask for a temporary sponsor at my first meeting. Then by my sixth meeting I will ask someone to be my permanent sponsor. I will call that sponsor every day just to get into the habit of talking to him, so that when I run into trouble, I will already have the habit of calling and talking".

Another part of the plan is to share at the meetings that are attended. It is one thing to go to a meeting, but quite another to take the risk of sharing something personal at that meeting. The more risk, the quicker and better the recovery. An addicted person can soak up a lot of wisdom by sitting and listening at the meetings, but eventually every sponge needs to be wrung out and that is where the sharing comes in.

The plan should include regular readings from educational and inspirational recovery materials. Each day should start with the proscribed reading in the "One Day at a Time" book, which includes a thought for the day, prayer for the day and a meditation for the day. I have suggested to patients in treatment that they should keep their little book on the back of the toilet. That way they can sit on the toilet and read as they start their day. It is like a complete cycle - they have good stuff going in one end from their readings and bad stuff going out the other end!

Obviously, the Big Book of Alcoholics Anonymous and Narcotics Anonymous should be read many times from cover to cover and there is a wealth of recovery literature available now for daily readings as well. Some people like to do religious readings as well, such as from the Bible, Torah or Quran.

Many times a successful program will include further outpatient counseling for specific issues such as: sexual abuse, Post Traumatic Stress Syndrome and marital discord.

A program of recovery should also include learning how to have fun without doing drugs. Many relapses happen simply because an addict doesn't know what to do with their time and doesn't know how to create fun in life. They end up thinking, "Well, my using got me in trouble, but at least it wasn't boring."

Recovery really comes down to determining to what lengths a person is willing to go to have something great later on. An example that I have used in group therapy with patients is to tell them that exactly 24 hours after this moment if they can prove through blood tests that they have been clean and sober for that 24 hour period then I will give them a million dollars. Then I ask them what they are willing to do to ensure that tomorrow at this same time, they will get their million bucks. Most of the time the group members will say something like, "Well, I just wouldn't drink or do drugs. But again, that doesn't really answer the question. To not drink or do drugs is the goal, but the question really is this: To what lengths are you willing to go to get the million"?

I then tell them that if they were to make me that offer, I would chain myself to the radiator and hire two armed guards with sawed-off shotguns. I would tell the guards that if I made a move to get out and go to the liquor store, they should blow my dang head off. I would also ask my sponsor to sit with me and read out of the Big Book of Alcoholics Anonymous until the next day. Now all of that sounds rather extreme and just a little bit bizarre, but it does give the right flavor of the lengths addicts might have to go to in order to get something that is far more valuable than a million dollars, namely, their recovery and their life.

Having a program of recovery is more than a wish or a hope or a desire. It is having a plan with measureable and observable actions that lead to the goal of recovery.

20

Prevention

It certainly would seem to be a better idea to prevent addictions in the first place rather than wait and then try to recover from an addiction. On my good days I think that might be possible, but on my bad days I doubt it.

In the first place, people usually start addictive behaviors when they are young and young people don't have enough life experience to know how things might turn out later on from their present behavior. Furthermore, as we talked about earlier, the first experiences that young people have with addictive substances are usually positive. Using chemicals makes young folks feel powerful, outgoing, witty and sexy, so what's not to like? The negative consequences usually only happen much later and by then the person has already come to depend on the effects of those addictive agents.

In addition, young people in this culture grow up believing that there is a quick-fix solution to everything and that things should come easily in this life. What could be easier to handle emotional problems than using something chemically to change the way one feels in a hurry? People are bombarded with advertising in all forms of media that constantly tell them that their particular product is the immediate solution to whatever problem they have.

So, that is why on my bad days, I really don't see that addiction can be prevented. But on other days, I see that although all addiction cannot be prevented, some addiction can be for some people and that is enough to do what we can to work towards that end.

One very important thing that parents can do is to make sure that they give family background about the disease of addiction to their children and let them know that addiction tends to run in families, just like other diseases. If a young woman knows that both of her grandmothers were alcoholics and that made her about 4 times more likely to lose control of alcohol if she used it, she might think twice about ever starting. Or, if a young Native American boy is informed that his people have almost no enzymatic resistance to alcohol, he might choose to never start drinking and live a healthy life.

This information about addiction should be given to offspring in a calm, concerned way just like information about other diseases is imparted. For example, both of my parents died of congestive heart failure and cancer, so I have told my children that these are diseases that they must be aware of and try to do the healthy things that can prevent these. I have also told them that their maternal grandfather was an alcoholic with some Native American background and thus, that makes them genetically predisposed to losing control of their drinking if they do very much of it.

It is surprising to me how many people have little or no idea what their genetic predisposition is for certain diseases and are caught unawares. Part of the problem has been that addiction has been seen as a shameful disease and families are reluctant to share anything with their children that they believe puts the family in a bad light and would shame them. But it is important for young people to know who they are and where they came from.

Another very important piece of the prevention puzzle is the example that parents set with their own attitudes about chemical usage. There is a saying concerning raising children that I have always liked.

It goes like this: "Our children will rarely listen to us, but they will never fail to imitate us". If parents are using chemicals irresponsibly, their children stand a very good chance to do exactly the same thing. It has never worked when parents tell their children, "Do as I say; not as I do". They do as we do. For example, telling your children to never smoke when you have a cigarette in your hand doesn't seem to carry much weight. Admonishing kids to stay off drugs when you are high never seems to do much for them either.

As parents we need to provide accurate information about chemicals and their abuse. We don't want to holler, scream or threaten, but just discuss in a calm, rational manner. We can't scare our children straight by telling them if they ever use their nose will fall off and they will drop over dead. They know that isn't true and that we are overreacting. But if we speak to them calmly about the seriousness of the consequences of chemical usage, it can help.

When children are allowed to suffer consequences for their actions, it usually makes them aware that they should think ahead to what consequences using drugs might have. If children have no responsibilities and suffer no consequences, why should they worry about doing whatever they want?

As I was growing up my father was a great one for being consistent in his discipline. I was never yelled at, was never hit and in fact, never had even one spanking in my entire life, but I had plenty of discipline. There were always consequences for my actions and I was made aware very clearly what these consequences would be. For example, I was doing a poor job of taking care of my 4-H cattle. There was manure in the feed bunk, the pen was messy and the water was dirty. My father came and checked up on this from time to time and found my care lacking. He said to me very calmly, "Kal, do you not want to take care of those cattle"? "Yeah", I said, "I'm taking care of them". "No, you're not. Look at the feed bunk and the water. You are just throwing some feed at them and then running to play. If you don't want to feed them, that's alright. Just let me know. I'll feed them and then I'll take the money for them when they are sold". There was not one part of me that doubted that he would do that very thing, because he always said what he meant and meant what he said. I learned about consequences in this way and it made me think twice about other areas of my life and what could happen.

It is important for parents to give positive attention to children rather than just negative attention. We must not wait until our children screw up and then jump on them. We must try to catch them doing something good and then praise them for it. Children want to please us if we give them half a chance and if they can respect us at all. They will live up to our expectations if they get positive attention along the way. We have a sign hanging on our kitchen wall that says, "There is nothing that sharpens a child's hearing like praise".

When my son was growing older he became big enough to mow the lawn and I was all excited about that. However, he would always wait for me to tell him that it was time to mow the lawn and I wanted him to just take this task over and do it without being told. Finally, I decided that I knew better parenting than I was doing and I sat him down and explained that everybody in our family had jobs to do. His was to do his homework, clean his room and mow the lawn. I told him that I expected him to be responsible and do these things without me having to ride his trail about it. Then I waited. The lawn was getting longer, but I was not going to remind him about it. I waited and almost chewed my fingers off while waiting. But finally, he mowed the lawn without being told. I then praised him to high heaven and told him "I am very pleased with the responsibility you are taking with the lawn. This is the kind of thing that I will remember when you get a little older and want to use the family car." I never had to say a word about the lawn again. Responsibility is a strong preventative factor for addiction.

Parents should always be united in their approach with their children and they should always be consistent. Children will try to divide and conquer with their parents if they think they can get their own way and it spoils them. Also, if discipline is not consistent it leads to insecurity in children and a feeling like insecurity is something for which chemicals are used as a cover up. Parents can use different parenting styles from strict to permissive if they are consistent in what they do.

Parents should assume that despite their best efforts, their children will most likely begin some experimentation at some time with drugs and alcohol. They should look for signs of using if things don't seem quite right and be prepared to discuss those concerns openly with the child.

One of the greatest things parents can do to help prevent addiction in their children is to encourage their children to share their feelings. They should be asking not just what their children think, but how they feel. The parents should set a good example by regularly sharing their own feelings, using feeling words. Examples of using feeling words would be the following: "I felt hurt today when my co-workers were going shopping after work and they did not invite me". "I was irritated when the boss let everybody choose their holiday time off except me". "I was scared when I saw the report that said our company was going to have to cut some staff and I thought it might be me."

Since it is true that chemical usage is all about taking care of feelings in an artificial way, then it is paramount that people learn how to handle feelings in a natural way if addiction is to be prevented. For most of us, it is not what happens to us in life that makes a difference. It is how we feel about what happens to us that is important. If we can handle our feelings immediately and appropriately there is a good chance for chemical health and mental health.

We have discussed prevention mainly for young people, but as we said before, there are a lot of older people, particularly senior citizens who are taking prescription medications that are addictive. Prevention for senior citizens means asking more questions of their physician as to whether or not a drug is habit-forming and if there is an alternative to taking this medication. Even taking an addictive medicine as prescribed will not stop dependency, so elderly people and their family members must be very careful with all medicines. There are natural methods of dealing with pain such as biofeedback, massage, yoga and other techniques rather than drugs.

In summary, although there is no way that all addictions can be prevented, there are things that can be done to help prevent them for many people. As the old saying goes, "An ounce of prevention is worth a pound of cure".

21

Working with addicts

For those of you that work with addicted persons either as a mental health professional, other professional, or simply as a family member or friend, there are some things to remember that will make your work go better.

It bears repeating that the addict needs to get the sense that you view them as "sick" and not as being "bad". Sick is treatable, but bad is to the bone as the song goes. A sick person may have some bad behaviors, but that is only a symptom of the sickness. An example that I have used in group at the treatment center is to have the patients imagine that someone in their family is sick with some strain of stomach flu. "How can you tell if you have stomach flu", I ask? "You will have vomiting, diarrhea and fever", they respond. "Would you be angry with that person if they vomited all over your rug on their way to the bathroom? What if they didn't make it to the toilet? Would you be mad"? "No, of course not", they reply. "They couldn't help themselves". Next, I ask them to imagine that their family member stood in the middle of their living room and stuck 3 fingers down their throat until they vomited on the rug. "Would you be mad then"? "Yes, we would be mad", they reply vehemently. "Well, what is the difference? In both cases the stain is the same and the smell is the same".

"Because the first person was sick and the second was just mean", the patients respond.

At this point we can look at some of the behaviors that the addicted persons have had and be honest about how much wreckage they have caused, but drop off some of the guilt about these behaviors, because they can see that they were sick and not just bad or mean. The addictive disease does cause a loss of values and a lowering of moral standards, but if the resultant behaviors can be recognized as part of the sickness, they can be accepted and forgiven much more readily.

One of the reasons that addicted persons tell so many lies is because they already see themselves as "bad" and don't want people to find out any other bad things about them and feel worse. We used to have a saying at the treatment center that went like this: "Do you want to be able to tell when an addict is lying to you? Their mouth is moving." Addicts gets so used to covering up, making excuses and blaming other people that they can actually lose the ability to distinguish what is the truth. We talked about denial earlier as the main symptom of the disease, but what becomes even worse is when denial slops over and becomes delusion. The distinction between denial and delusion is that denial is a lie to protect one's image, but the liar knows it's a lie. Delusion is when the liar actually believes himself and can be as convincing as only someone who is themselves convinced can be. Another way of saying this is that denial is the bull crap you tell somebody else, but you know it is bull crap. Delusion is when you actually believe your own bull crap! No wonder addicts can lie so convincingly.

A recovering colleague of mine when I worked at the outpatient clinic told the story of dishonesty in his own recovery. He said that he and his wife lived in a house with the garage out back that was entered from the alley. They had new neighbors move in and he introduced himself over the fence behind the garage to this new man. After a lengthy chat he went back in the house and his wife asked him where he had been all that time. Before he could stop himself he said, "Oh, I had to run downtown for a pack of cigarettes". A little later he confessed his lie to his wife. There was no need for him to lie. He wasn't doing anything wrong and was in fact being a good neighbor. He even told the neighbor that he was a recovering addict for the past 2 years. It is a telling fact that even after this amount of continuous sobriety a lie would come to him quicker than the truth even when the truth would have served better!

Because of this tendency there are many times when dishonesty has to be confronted if you are to do any good working with addicts. But we always need to remember the difference between confronting and condemning. As we said at the outset, if an addict gets one whiff of condemnation from you, you are finished. At some point your addicted client will probably be mad at you because you do confront their sick behaviors, but if they know it is about the behavior and not the person, they will get over it. In fact, if there is not some point at which an addict is mad, you are probably not doing your job.

I have a little story that I sometimes tell patients early on in therapy that helps them accept the honest confronting that needs to happen in recovery. Here is the story. Once upon a time there was a little sparrow that lived in a dairy barn in Minnesota. It was winter and the temperature was 30 degrees below zero. The little sparrow needed a drink in the morning and dropped down onto the cattle water tank, but slipped on the ice and was submerged in the water. He flopped out onto the ground, but was so cold he couldn't fly, so he hopped out of the barn into the pasture to avoid getting stomped by the cows. He could go no further and was frozen solid. By chance a big Holstein cow walked over him and barely avoided stepping on him. She stopped right in front of him and hunched up and dropped a big steaming pile of "cow flopper" on the little bird. This seems like a nasty thing, but it was hot and warmed the little bird up and he was able to move around again, so it actually helped. The movement attracted the attention of a coyote lurking on the edge of the pasture. The coyote came over and scraped the cow dung off the little bird – and then he ate him! The moral of the story is that not everybody who appears to be crapping on you is your enemy and not everybody who appears to be scraping crap off you is your friend!

A sense of humor can go a long way in working with addicts. They need to know that you are taking them seriously, but not taking yourself too seriously. If one of the spiritual goals is for the addict to gain humility, then it is important for them to be able to laugh at themselves, for that is the beginning of humility. There is a big difference between humility and humiliation. Humility is basically just honesty; being able to say that this is who I am and that is alright, because I am getting better. Humiliation is something only the individual can do to themselves in saying that they are not alright and never will be.

To be effective in working with addicted persons one must be able to both confront and support them. There are some people who can really confront and can blow somebody out of the water in a heartbeat, but they are not very supportive. There are also other people who are very good at supporting. They are nurturing, caring and concerned, but have trouble leveling with another. But to really help to bring change to an addict one must be able to confront sick behaviors when they happen and then turn right around on a dime and support healthy behaviors when they take place.

Many physicians, nurses and counselors don't really like working with addicts, because they lie to them and don't do what is suggested. If you can get past these nasty symptoms of the disease and remember that they are just symptoms, you can help. There is a great reward in helping people with a fatal disease get well and be extraordinary recovering people.

Conclusion

When one considers not only the huge number of persons who are afflicted with addictions, but add in the people who are affected by these persons with addictions, it becomes evident that we are all in trouble in our culture. In fact, it is not too bold a statement to say that addiction is our most pressing health issue today. It has been estimated that a full one-third of all patients in any general hospital are there either directly or indirectly because of addictions. If that is true, and my experience in the hospital tells me it is, then it would seem natural that we devote ourselves to understanding this disease and working towards the healing of it.

It is not only ironic, but sad that as this problem grows, the resources towards helping with recovery have actually dwindled. Treatment centers have been closed, clinics have stopped dealing with addictions and money designated for assisting recovery has dried up. Insurance companies that used to regularly pay for a 28 day inpatient treatment stay have either totally done away with coverage of addictions or have reduced coverage to a few outpatient appointments.

Until addiction takes its rightful place alongside all other diseases in the public's mind, this problem will continue. If public perception continues to be that addiction is "not really a disease", but is a "moral failure" brought upon oneself and therefore not deserving of any help or financial support, then this health problem will only get worse.

Likewise, if our culture continues on its present path of looking for quick-fix and easy-fix solutions for everything, especially when it comes to dealing with any painful feelings, we will end up with more of the same. People sometimes ask me what I think would have to happen to help the drug crisis in our culture and I can't say for certain. But I do think that it would take a spiritual renewal of our entire culture to have any lasting effect. We would have to come to believe that some pain is necessary in life and that we can handle it naturally. We would have to learn how to express feelings immediately and appropriately from an early age on. We would have to educate our children concerning the genetic predisposition that they have for losing control of addictive agents. We would have to view addiction like any other disease and drop the shame off concerning the illness. We would have to address addiction problems much earlier with an individual. We would have to let folks know that there is joy in recovery, not just pain.

Addiction is a disease that is "cunning, baffling and powerful", and will always be cunning and powerful, but hopefully this book has made it a little less baffling and a little more understandable.

To all of you that are in recovery, you have my admiration. To all of you that need recovery, you have my pledge that there is a better spiritual way to live out there waiting for you. To all who have been affected by the disease, you have my sympathy, but also my assurance that you can overcome. To all who are still perplexed by addiction, read more, talk more and listen more. Addiction makes sense in a sick sort of way once you understand it.

CPSIA information can be obtained
at www.ICGtesting.com
Printed in the USA
FSHW04n2200190418
47206FS